Death Fluorescence

Copyright © 2025 by Julia Bouwsma
ISBN: 978-1-951979-83-6
Library of Congress: 2025934120
Published by Sundress Publications
www.sundresspublications.com

Book Editor: Ada Wofford
Managing Editor: Krista Cox
Editorial Assistant: Kanika Lawton
Editorial Interns: Mia Grace Davis, Jahmayla Pointer, Annabel Phoel

Colophon: This book is set in Cormorant.

Cover Image: "Abyss" by Beth Conklin
Cover Design: Kristen Camille Ton
Book Design: Krista Cox

Death Fluorescence
Julia Bouwsma

for my grandmothers, both lovers of language—

Contents

Hiraeth 13
Sugaring at the Start of Another War 14
Blood and Soil 15
After We Wound the Land to Maps 17
Point of Origin 19
Diaspora 20
Haunt 21
Etymology of Land 22
A Meditation on Parasitic Infection 27
Study in Epigenetic Memory: A Memory of Warmth 30

I'm Okay, but the Country Is Not 33

Self-Portrait as the Shadow, the Vessel, and the Broken Handle . . 51
My Acupuncturist Tells Me to Have a Conversation with My Pain . . 53
Study in Epigenetic Memory: The Neurosis Persists 55
The Thing About Fire 58
Screw Self-Care 59
Muscle Memory: A Surgery 61

Small-Town Parade / Frozen Lake: Notes on Fear 71

Drought Diary 91
I Have No Answer but Stones 92
A Catalog of Endlings 93
Home Movie with Storm, Orchard, and News 95
Dream with Jericho Brown, Peaches, and Grief 97
What Will You Do at the End of the World? 98
The Book on Self-Compassion 99

To a Mainer Living 100 Years from Now 103
Further Notes on Fear 104
Beauty Standards Have Fallen Under Lockdown 106

What's Efflorescing We've Been Afraid to Say 107
Study in Epigenetic Memory: Flower and Petal 108
Elegy for My Grandmother in the Form of a Cactus 109
Blessing for the End Times 111
Death Fluorescence 112

Notes 115
Acknowledgments 117

*It is not you who will speak; let the disaster speak in you,
even if it be by your forgetfulness or silence.*

—Maurice Blanchot

*You must speak to it till your voice
catches the thread of all sorrows
and you see the size of the cloth.*

—Naomi Shihab Nye

Hiraeth

Each night I dream our land inside out:
        backwards roads thread the woods. At the wrong
                angles: field and mud. Where trees should be

the exposure swivels without warning. The hill
        rises taller: a turned-down mouth of rock and ledge.
                Each familiar suddenly unfamiliar, I run

the road below the house. I drag a leash with no dog.
        I hike the back trail and the non-dog at my side
                becomes a dog, becomes a coyote, leaps its manged

flash into night. Air so thick I could drink it. I snowmobile
        the back loop: the trail unfurls into a pack of wolves.
                I slow the throttle, I pass through them, dream-numb,

ready to embrace my fate. I return to our house
        and you have made a fire pit of cinder blocks on the floor
                where the kitchen table should be. You turn

and offer me a sausage, a stick. Sheet plastic flaps
        where windows were. There are trucks I don't recognize
                parked on the lawn and the garden is heavy with mulch hay

I never laid down. The cauliflowers rot. The tomatoes
        have frozen orange on the vine. Drunk in the morning:
                this shame at being lost in a house my own

two hands have built. A door leads out back to a slate patio,
        a frog pond bloating the silhouette of a child. I wake
                into the fear of my body. Muddled bedsheets

sweat our bodies together and I reach out to trace
        the juncture, slicked, where your hip bone meets mine.
                Gentle: I am reading a map. Show me a route that doesn't

twist on itself. Teach me to live here without regret.

Sugaring at the Start of Another War

> *The tree of liberty must be refreshed from time to time with the blood of patriots & tyrants. It is its natural manure.*
> —Thomas Jefferson

This year it's all melt and bleed. The moon hemorrhages
through the branches—dancing out of season with her red frock—
and we know what it means: when the world around you is
dying, practice with your hands. Dress for combat. It's time

to tap the trees again, time to hang the buckets for the sweet
let-down. You drill the maples. I hammer spiles into fresh
wounds. The trees spout, they mouth-drip. It's nothing new,
this brew we boil of our collective sorrow. We do it every spring,

but this year I am measuring dread more precisely than before.
Now I am all metaphor and chewed lips—a sleepless anxiety that coils
and recoils my skin, finds me trembling in the strangest places.
The dentist's chair, for example, where she bends toward my

open mouth, smiles, and sweetly declares, *We're stockpiling guns.
When the time comes, we'll be ready to fight. We just don't know how yet,
or whom.* She switches the dremel on, metal whine hungry
as a swarm, and grinds the stain from the backs of my teeth.

Everyone here is gingerly unspooling risk, all of us trying on
words in secret—*underground railroad, soldier, fascism, courage, refuse*—
inherited language as suddenly alien as unlabeled boxes
in a dead grandmother's closet: ornate Cyrillic carved

into a samovar's golden flourish, the unknown ancestor
who scowls through beard and fez at the photographer's lens,
an amateur oil painting of a woman stooped before her hoe
to the work of the field. None of us understands what it means,

but we bend throat to throat with the trees and drink hard,
pull away and watch the sap spill out over our palms. We all know
it runs clear every spring, until it doesn't. Even those of us who don't
believe in fear or souls remember there's sugar in blood.

Blood and Soil

Charlottesville, Virginia, August 2017

NPR is playing in my back pocket, has been all morning
as I bend and crawl, clawing pigweed and purslane and thistle,
tearing yellowed, mildewed leaves from the tomatoes.
Black spots on some and brittled brown as insect shells on a windowsill.
I worry about blight, never know if it's safe to compost the trimmings.
All that heat will fester disease, keep it warm through the winter
until it comes back stronger next year. The journalists
are so careful with their words, I wonder if they fear the same:
Alt-right, white nationalist, they say. Never *white supremacy, neo-Nazis, KKK*.
I wipe my hands off on the ass of my jeans, bundle a clutch of cucumbers
into the gray billow of my T-shirt. My fingernails are gaumed up with dirt,
slug slime, the green juice the tomato vines bleed when you rip
them at the stem—sticky-tack stubborn as tobacco spit.

Back in the kitchen, earth crusts freshly-split hangnails I peel
then watch as they trickle crimson into muddy sink-water.
Scrub each finger three times with the potato brush.
From my back pocket a clip of the crowd, now rhythmic with frenzy,
torches in their fists as they chant: *Blood and soil. Blood and soil.*
Each word is spit-shined, each word drops a black boot into my stomach,
a familiar unfamiliar chill. *Blood and soil:* what I'm washing from my hands
right now, this garden I've spent all morning in, this land I've worked
to bone and cracked palm. I've bled into the mud and the mud has bled
into my skin, has laid rows of tiny scars like a language I still carry in my flesh
though I've forgotten how to speak it. Before me, this land was someone else's
—Land of the Dawn stolen from the People of the Dawn—and when I die

it will be someone else's again: a cycle as fixed as seasons, as deep
as this clay and ledge. At fifteen my great-grandmother sang alphabets
of departure as she and her sisters filled suitcases, as they folded,
smoothed, pressed. Her family had a farm in Ukraine or Austria or Poland,
or was it a vodka distillery—each version flecks out from the mouth
of the teller, borderless, each telling a droplet cast in another direction—
the land perhaps theirs or perhaps not, according to those who say they weren't
allowed to own. *Blood*: what's matted into the young man's cornrows after
he's beaten with metal poles in a parking garage. *Soil*: the bowels release
involuntarily when you die. The car plows through bodies like a tractor
through a wheat field, reaps another harvest of blood. They left their land
for the city, they left the city for the sea.

On the radio, another young man is stating his three reasons
for attending the rally, and the third is: *Kill as many Jews as possible*.
Sow the same crop year after year and the soil will starve, plants grow thin
and sallow—blister and shrivel until there's nothing left to harvest, nothing
to eat. I can't read the language on the passports nor recognize
a single face in photographs. I don't even know my great-grandmother's
birth name. But the taste of earth is on my lips. The soil maps
a dirt-slicked path across my palm. From my kitchen window, I see
horizon stitch a ghost-bleach sky, see it beckon with its long gray scar
from that unknown farm to mine in Maine—as those who fled
to bring me here once stood on ship decks and watched their home
unfurl into blurred shorelines, their bodies slacking and cinching,
now empty as flour sacks, now tight as a fistful of stones.

After We Wound the Land to Maps

Better *stewardship* than *ownership*, but this wooded hill has never
needed anyone. Without us, it stretched its green flanks feral
until blackberry canes cracked under their own weight, deer tramped
switchback tunnels through the undergrowth, columbine erupted
purple and pink-white beneath sugar maples. Without us, the hill's
scars turned porous: August aster bottlebrushed from cellar holes,
a stand of ash rose from a single stump, snakes studded
themselves into the splicing silences of the stone walls and slept.
Without us, the stories grew moss and sprouted saplings
like an erratic boulder from its hulking granite back. And likely
the hill preferred this, for it never needed us here to hear or tell
of the seven-sided pole barn filled with its seven years of trash,
of the baby diapers and propane tanks that shot shrapnel
when the man before us set it ablaze. Nor did it need the story
of the DEA helicopter sent to arrest the man before him, man
of shotgun and wild rumors, of holes all over the front lawn
where the pot plants grew and where we still now sometimes stumble
carrying our buckets. No, the land didn't need the herd of cows
before him either, or the family they belonged to, the ones who built
this rotting cabin, who dug septic and well and then one day just up
and disappeared. Though that woman came back once, in a dusty white
minivan driven by her daughter, came to see one last time her lost
home and told me—through plastic oxygen tubes from the car window—
of a time when this whole hillside rolled with wheat, sheep, fields
and the hubris of a farmer who scrambled to gather his hay as thunderclouds
bore down upon him, how once the last bale was in, he shook his fist
at the sky in triumph and the sky replied a pitchfork of lightning
right into the roof of his barn. So fire. So all those fields regrew to woods.

So new scrub for the partridge. So no trace of the now-vanished schoolhouse,
nothing left of the sawmill but a clogged stone dam and a swamp
of dank leaves. Just the headstones remain: mildew and algae on marble,
children buried before their parents. Just the rusted gate, the tree-bent
chain link. The rest left home at first opportunity, drawn by the heady
violence of opportunity, abandoned this hill to a new violence of boundary
pins and parceling out. And now I am here, an unwanted steward, unneeded
witness. I am here, and this topography has made a debt of me. The debt
began before we ever arrived. Perhaps the debt began when someone
followed a deer through the woods on the way to the river. Or perhaps
when the mountains first churned with glacial debris. Certainly the debt
began when someone wrote their name on a property map, a deed.
And by the time we arrived, adolescent on the solipsistic romance
of our own manifest destiny, believing we could make our own end,
glowing from the flickering light of flame-colored leaves, we already knew:
the wound was us. It lodged in our throats, it grew under our tongues—
moss to a slope, lily of the valley to a grave—until we could no longer
discern the green of the hill from the skin of our hands. Each spring
weeps its spring runoff, sugars the trees with tears, but the wound
remains. The wound festers violet and lilac; it swells a bloat-pond
of summer warbling; it lacerates a hot fist of fall color with the urgency
of an extinction burst, and yet the land lumbers on—its low dirge of survival
and pine pitch stitching us—lichen to lesion, light to ligament, rock to rib.

Point of Origin

Discussing the problem of origins with my mother on the telephone
again, I watch the frozen lake extend beneath the windowpanes.
A frozen lake recalls blank poster board as in grade school—half the family tree
wizened white after I came home asking nationalities, countries of origin
and my mother said, *Just put Jewish* and I said, *Jewish is not a country*
so she tried to tell me what she knew, which amounted to something like snow
falling in a forest that spanned all the way from Austria to Lithuania or Estonia
or Russia, a forest marked by sudden uneven clearings called fields where
bodies might be found, a dark forest pocked by villages no one wanted
to remember the names of so they forgot them or in any event forgot to tell
their children as perhaps they forgot even their own names, stilled and severed
until it became impossible to trace: one name found on a ship's manifest, another
claimed at entry, a stranger inside a familiar, a matryoshka we don't speak of until
it's too late, the ones who know now dead and gone, the documents scattered
and opaque. On the phone my mother speaks of research, suggests a distant relative
who might know more, but like the crusted snow that coats this lake, erasure
has become a skin. Inside me an expanse of ice extends and below that ice
a fish swims slow and dark, scaling figure eights between the stones. In winter
a lake transforms to field. Between pickup trucks and fishing shacks, a lone figure
paces. I cannot see the fish, and yet I know it's there, beneath this makeshift ground.

Diaspora

I open my fist, and a flight of sparrows releases—
my breath lifts up, dispelling
droplets. The droplets grow wings and circle
the dunes. My grandmother wrote about this
on the hospital windowsill, her words marching
like crooked ants from radiator to sand-colored wall.

Dislocation: I stand outside myself to watch my grandmother
write. Her words could be our ancestors divided
into two straight marching lines. I betray myself
so often. Yesterday I apologized for not knowing
what I should have known if this town
were my home. It is not my home.
I blamed the asker. I blamed myself.

Haunt

it only took
one night
in the twin four-poster beds
our grandmother chose
in the house that was a stop
house with a secret
across the hall
where we never again slept
where our bodies
were a catalog
of relentless hours
staring upward
stick-on stars
cast
down onto
blue cornflowers
hydroponic
with darkness
indigo
sky
the trim boards
buckled
to our terror
the hair ribbon pulled
our eyes
open wide
our silence

my sister and I
in the blue-doored room
under matching duvets
in the old part of the farmhouse
on the Underground Railroad
a secret staircase
from our room
where we laid awake
wormed with secrets
cell by cell
pupils pinned
to a galaxy of glowing
new moons
green light
our faces
sprouted
flowers that fed
and crawled
along the walls
eating
the floorboards
as we lay fixed
constellated
loose against
a nocturnal ceiling
our throats
howled a nebula

Etymology of Land

1. *ground, soil*

> May-born, I carry a low grime beneath my fingernails. Lineage swings its pickaxe
>
> to the ground. Stroke after stroke, it refuses to lift its head. I come from a people ordered to dig our own graves. My first instinct is to flee
>
> to the garden. My first instinct is to close my eyes, tell myself, *This is your bed. Now lie in it.* Before this land, my body was my first terrain, a soft yielding to dig and blade. Mud that squelches lets anyone in. I did not remember my shape
>
> and so I could not reclaim my shape, my body an emptiness I brought with me everywhere. Numb, without roots, I was always making myself a geography for someone else. The only alternative
>
> is to run. How quickly our bodies become the rituals required to leave it— a gathering of keys, a slamming of doors.

2. *the surface of the earth and all its natural resources—*

> Because I was raised on the old ballads. Because my father's drunken mouth sang hills and riverbanks as archetype whiskeyed his teeth, softened
>
> his bones. Because moonshine shimmers the river white. Because the man standing beside his lover on the bank will never escape the circle his fingers make as they wrap her throat and tighten.
>
> Turn flesh. Turn moonlight. It's under here somewhere. Turn blood. Turn soil. I learned the words to all the songs. Later, to fill in the blank spots, I mixed them up, mixed them together.

3. *definite portion of the earth's surface, home region of a person or a people, territory marked by political boundaries*

    Auntie insists there's no difference between shit and mud.
    It's all caca to me, she says. Because we

    are not the only ones. Driven, driving. This hard rain.
    This open-mouthed rubble still falling—

    where a grave could be called a home. And a skin
    could be called a grave.

    And an archeological excavation site is long enough
    to lie down flat inside, arms crisscrossed over your chest.

    Consider me a surveyor then. Razor blades my plumb rule.

    The familiars of fence posts are scars. The familiars
    of blood, tendons, nerves are hardpan clay, root rot, grubs.

    Consider me cartographer. I was only drawing a map.

    Yellow fat under the thigh. I cut. I dug. What you can't forget
    and can't recall,

    you furrow. Consider me farmer.

4. *the solid part of the surface of the earth—*

    This *here* then, this wooded hilltop, where I rut myself across the surface

    until the surface ruts me. Where I open and blackfly. Where I all sweat
    and waistband. Where I bend and bend and the earth

    like the open page bends, red and knotted, back. And all our ghosts
    like the earth bend, red and knotted, back.

5. *an open space*

        Our meeting place, our confluence: Here we steel ourselves for love
        and everything we love is stolen. Here the labor never ends, our feet
        not the first nor the last. We practice becoming *solid*. We dig
        our spade in, dig our hands in. Sink or claw. Chop

        then wobble our weight against the blade. Hack at the roots. Plant
        the crop. When it blights, spoils, plant it again. Here it doesn't take long

        to hit clay. To hit the sticking point. The gray, the hard, the edge
        of memory, the salt taste like skin peeling the runnels
        of our mouths as we work—

6. *enclosure, church*

        What is the opposite of confession? This whole hillside
        bleeds water. I spill at the edges, suffer a loose tongue, but I'm not
        asking for forgiveness. My love tells me he's dry as a well

        in summer drought. He chisels and sands the spine of each beam
        for our house, back bent to the rhythm of his hands. He pops another beer,
        creases his mouth shut. I know there's a dark well thrumming beneath
        his organs, artesian. The dog bites the other dog and after staples,
        antibiotics, we assume she's fine. Only two years later do we find it—
        a hard lump. Infection walls itself off

        corner by corner, post by post. This hardness becomes our home.

        This hardness holds us close.

7. *"fallow land"*

    Lupine, also known as blue bonnet, is poisonous to sheep, cattle, horses, dogs.
    Our neighbor loathes them so I dig his up, replant them in my own yard
    where they wither without water.

    Each night it rains a dirge of torn sheets. In dreams I let myself go, wander
    naked as the pocked moon, round as a bloated tick. My fat and hang
    lead the way. I am always running—shame an afterthought

    to the tangle of tongue in hair. A feral singing through the trees,
    the taste in my mouth like a substratum

    I wake from, scent of loam still on my teeth.

8. *"wasteland"*

    Story says this is how our hill was born: a girl wandering the woods
    found a soft spot to bury a sorrow. A sorrow swells just as well in hardpan
    or loam. This one grew between rock and bone. Grew like tumor or longing
    or absence. Grew like a child, skull pointed toward the rusted gate. Grew
    like maple roots creeping, like fingers,

    apple blossoms in a clutch of branch, a silence tucked into another silence,
    flat and wide and hollow as dry rot. This sorrow
    grows until it's just a space where a sorrow used to be—

    worms in, worms out. In winter it folds

    its naked self over itself

    until the cabin posts heave and the doors won't open right,
    won't close.

9. *in the American English exclamation "land's sakes," land is a euphemism for Lord*

> I walk restless until my steps become the road.
>
> Each spring the mud belly-ups a new harvest of trash: bottle of piss, shirt sleeve, tarnished silver spoon, old man's face translucent on the delaminated film of a lost driver's license. This land is riddled
>
> with the expunged. We all walk on carcass and jawbone, a fist of chewing beetles. We all sink our shovels in and slice another cache of dust. This land is abscess we refuse to drain. This pus this blood this rock this tooth
>
> it mines us.
>
> Let it.

A Meditation on Parasitic Infection

> *Ascaris suum, also called the large pig roundworm or the large white worm, is a species of parasitic roundworm that infects pigs and wild boars worldwide. Cousin to the giant A. suum is the microscopic* Caenorhabditis elegans *nematode. C. elegans is notable for the singular blue light it emits at expiry, a phenomenon known as "death fluorescence."*

The long-lashed almost-human orb
      of the pig's eye swivels into a white squeal

of panic, wheelbarrowing as I grab the shoat's
      hocks firm and don't let go until the syringe

pierces flesh and all the Ivermectin empties
      beneath the skin of his straining neck.

When a pig begins to cough, we know
      there are worms in the lungs. Untreated,

an infestation will cause pneumonia, hepatitis,
      a general condition of wasting

known as *ill thrift*. But, of course, facts like this don't
      change anything. It's my job to hold on. A pig

will fight hard to get away from me. It's my job
      to hold tight, knuckles locking

as I bring this around to the matter at hand
      which is how beautiful our fear can look—

conjunctivitis bluing the pig's eye to gemstone:
      Milky Aquamarine, Fire Opal, Selenite,

Angelite, always some glowing jewel at the heart
        of the damage we carry, the pain we pass on

without intention, hurt carried deep inside
        ourselves, so often invisible until

it isn't. Like that time I looked down
        before I flushed and saw my shit

had a writhing white tail—
        that's what I mean, what I want

to talk about, the kind of shame you can't
        shake no matter how hard you scrub

under your fingernails, no matter that
        one sixth of the world's population

is carrying it too, *Ascaris suum*, roundworm,
        hidden everywhere in the earth

we're all living on each day, a natural cycle
        of spring rain and mud, eggs transferred

in the soft dark heart of the soil
        or found clinging to plant matter—

the harm we harbor in our own bodies
        without knowing, the hosts we become,

unexpected homes for *pathogens*,
        word the vet utters on the phone

after a week of pneumonia, Penicillin
        injections, the piglet refusing food

and water, weakening as his tail uncurls
        and flies gather along seeping lids,

until the vet says, *You've done all you can,*
        and there's nothing else left

but the gun and the thrash,
        the grain sack and the stain

that oozes now with its warm stink
        of bloodshitflesh as I tender

my naked legs through blackberry canes
        to set the piglet beneath the leaves

and leave him there
        for the coyotes to feed,

standing among the bramble, wondering
        how did we get here and how

do I trace our way back, hands
        quaking, my own eyes wheeling

brown as rot, searching for
        something, anything to string

us all back together, string some beauty
        to this mess, some light, any light

so blue, so brilliant, it's like the sky
        has swallowed the earth.

Study in Epigenetic Memory: A Memory of Warmth

Researchers have manipulated the C. elegans *nematode to produce a fluorescent protein, which creates a distinct green glow when the worm is transported to warmer climates. When returned to its native cold, this glow remains for up to fourteen generations.*

This map of earth makes a bright light we stare at our wound and what it does to us say we all know the scrape of it the belly-dark of it say it's not the cold we were hardened for but the sudden warmth that wounds us say our wound and theirs and theirs and theirs and their children and theirs and theirs and theirs through yet another clutch of earth how that memory of once-warmth guides even our children and theirs and theirs and theirs

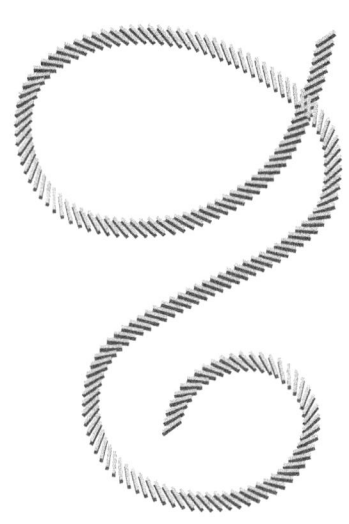

I'm Okay, but the Country Is Not

I'm okay, but the country is not, says my grandmother
before she dies, before she closes her eyes
and sleeps the sleep from which one does not rise.
Breath curdles what's left of the words in her,
the ocean her lungs will become. Drift downriver—
familiar current of language, swirling ink-stained skies,
but at the end, it's calm. A blanket unfurls. She lies
still, a raft in an eddy, cocooned in cotton departure.
On the far edge of the bed, a scarred shoreline waits.
There's a map of ruin inside each veined limb, trails
of bruises you can follow back. Once, a girl played
a finger piano in a white-collared dress, and spates
of curls exploded from her skull like scales
as she laughed at the music her own fingers made.

Follow the music her fingers made: this is how we slip
into memory. Laugh with her. This is how we fall.
I remember everything, she says, face to the wall,
it's a problem. Her voice is frayed, a leaking ship.
The newspapers pile up unread; she doesn't flip
a page. *Afraid:* the word she will not say, and yet we see
her see the people forgetting, unspooling a century,
how the fascia—invisible braid, coiling strip
that ties our tongues to our hearts—is tightening.
Never forget: pink membrane, shard of ash she taught
me to carry under it, sugar cube, our sweet defiance.
Now mouths hang open as we speak, even swallowing.
What Jew goes easy? She tosses, turns, is fitful, caught,
and not until the final day does she succumb to silence.

On the final day she succumbs to silence's drip,
but still—at her own funeral—she speaks. The rabbi
calls it a first. My uncle holds his iPhone up high,
and we huddle in close, listen as she recites with slurred lip
Carlyle, waterlogged lungs swimming to the sodden tip
of her tongue: *Here hath been dawning / Another blue day*
then, *Think, will thou let it / Slip useless away?*
I fold my printed, transliterated page of Kaddish, grip
these words I don't know, fold and fold until it is a white
square at the bottom of my pocket, promise or accusation
I hold tight to my fist. Later, in the dead winter leaf-
litter of my mother's yard, I scroll headlines, weep, bite
the riddle half-cracked in my cheek: *What slips and keeps on
slipping?* I am a hopeless clot of knuckles and grief.

Hopeless clot of knuckles and grief, a friend slips her
hand into mine. We walk two miles to the Lincoln
Memorial, we climb stone over stone over stone—
Lincoln towers above us, a pale and silent boulder.
His lips are Georgia marble now, left fist a quiver
of rage, right hand flat as sorrow. He's gone to bone.
Shoulders back, I try to be brave: *I am the captain
of my soul,* I thunder up to him. Henley for Grandfather,
Carlyle for her, but these poets are too dead for the dead,
and I'm drunk on gin, a trickle of pee in my tights. *I'm okay*—
it's a child's lie, a self-soothe, but maybe she just meant
we've no time left for private pain. We ancestors of the fled
who walk here on shadows of ghosts, turn our faces away
when we arrive, our iron shoes bolted to riverbank cement.

Iron shoes bolted to riverbank cement, or wherever
you left your dead—most of us can't name the spot,
absence a matryoshka, you open the doll and: naught.
Inside each emptiness is an emptiness and then another—
doll I was with dark eyes, in the arms of my grandmother
who loved me but carried my forgetting as a fraught
chain of shame (as does my mother still). *She does not
know her Jewish history*, she wrote of me while under
prednisone's sharp clasp, a frenzy of writing the first time
her kidneys failed: the eggshell of her hospital windowsill
crawling a cursive army of ballpoint ants. Language, it
spilled from her everywhere, anxious heat of the sublime,
her script tremored with effort, her words gathered as gravel
into a moraine I'll never slip: *and she has the résumé to prove it.*

Moraine as a résumé inside my bones, proof I'll never slip
too far away. Ruin we carry in our bodies, shame song
we pass through families, croon in rounds. Mutilation
reverberates in us cell by cell—stories you can't clip
the tails from. Take August Weismann's effort to snip
sixty-eight mice in an experiment five generations strong:
nine hundred and one pinkies, each with a tail as long
as the last, one amputation after another simply to strip
claims of Jews born without foreskins. Grandma, she
studied this in dusty libraries, through charts and diagrams,
diaries and portraits, the quest of men, their dogged work
to discover in the cell a material theory of heredity
in these sometimes bewildering times, in these breeched dams
of centuries, in this smooth space curve we're born to torque.

Smooth as the space we're born to, we torque the Möbius strip
of memory. Even before *helix* was a word, we uncoiled. Inside
each story my grandmother told there was another to elide,
and the silent stories echoed loudest. Now our stewardship
empties her house of all refrains. Another armful, another trip
to trash or car. Ruin banquets the floor. She leaves a landslide
of choruses behind: belly-sagging shelves, books we divide
and sort, towers of papers lining the study walls, a ship
in a bottle, her mother's tablecloth, mothballs in the folds,
every birthday card ever sent, a file marked *Julia* in the back
of the antique writing desk: poems, programs, the mute
manila pride that yellows in solitude, that quietly holds
me as we make arrangements, as we clean and pack,
our heels against the kitchen slate so high and resolute.

Our heels sing out against her kitchen slate: Take silverware,
the floral couch, blankets, that red vase I bought in Venice,
take the painting of the cobbler and his apprentice
in their gilded frame. Take it, even the blue dinner
plates. Each of her cells was made of words. Now her
words bore themselves into my skin. Body braids a noose
of lace, quivering rope of sinew and caul we can't cut loose.
Instead we pull taut, we let silence cinch us. Never
ever has it been okay. America is its own damaged DNA.
It circles in on itself until the throat catches inside the throat—
isn't, it *isn't.* All I've got is language now: what's sung,
what slips rain-stained, what spills my lips. Words, they
phalanx my fists with ink. And still she sleeps, slips. No quote
soothes my rage. Let me fall forever if I unstring my tongue—

Unstring, unstrung. It gives me comfort, our shared
loose tongue. I think before I speak, then stumble the spiral
staircase. Tumble down. Left foot, loose foot. The right's
to bite. A tablespoon's for eating tables with. The blue plate
shattered, then the coffee cup. I tried to glue it
before I threw it away. I write these poems to braid you
a daisy chain, twist you a helix of fairy lights, line your path
with brown-haired girls, their linked arms in fleur-de-lis
and silver snaps. But just look at these hands:
I'm shit with a tape measure, worse with a hammer.
Mornings I lie in my bed, rectangles on all sides,
and bang the walls with my fists. These sonnets
are not what I'd thought. I'm sorry I built you a box
when all I wanted was to blossom you back.

All I wanted was to blossom you back. You who once lost a year
swallowed to hospital, dialysis, wheelchair, walker, obedient
mouth opening for the spoon. You who were there-not-there.
We stuck honeysuckle under your nose and you opened
your eyes, mumbled *lovely*, closed again. We recited
poetry, Longfellow for the Fourth, acted out Paul Revere's ride,
pretended to gallop our imaginary horse. You who stayed
gone, shut tight. You who came back one day, just like that—
blinked twice, remembered nothing. Who smiled, girlish
and fierce, then declared the turkey too salty. You always
did talk too loud. Your hearing was shot. I egged you on
in public the last time I saw you, Election Day, lunch after
voting. *Horrible man*, you bellowed and the next table laughed,
but when the results came in all you said was, *I've seen this before.*

I've seen this before. One by one, the results come in:
first a mild stroke, next kidneys wither, a fascist bloviates
on the screen, a grandmother extends her left arm
to the phlebotomist's glove. A dark ocean of bruise gathers tidal
beneath her skin. Each morning's headlines are another fist. I wake
to the woodstove's cold belly and scrape the firebox clean.
Sunrise comes for me through the trees and her bright wound
demands: *Get up. Get dressed.* In the bathroom I bare my teeth
to the mirror, grip the porcelain. Familiar doesn't make easier.
But memory is a muscle. I let it hold me when my knees
go loose. Inheritance means I will bend and lace my boots,
I will pick up my shovel and teeter my blade into
frosted root rot. I will tuck late daffodil bulbs between
clay-packed stones. Some will die and some will bloom.

Some will die before spring and some will bloom ragged
and yellow, orange-frilled mouths hungry for a milder wind,
double heads cast in different directions. I weave the garden
rows, tending. I wander the rocky path and the thud
of my footsteps echoes me. Once I breathed in the sharp
green air and thought, *Work will set me free*. Then I recalled
the iron gates that spell these words, language like chromosomes
set deep in the bones. A hole is for digging. I dig you another
poem then descend into the poem to wait. Each hole leads
to another hole—half mitzvah, half grave. They gather in circles,
they helix the hillside. Half the time I'm afraid of where my feet
will take me. My mother furrows as she reads the news: *We're going
backwards*. I press my nose to the earth. Wherever we end up,
we'll bring our shovels. Wherever we go, there'll be music there.

Bring your shovel. Wherever we go, there'll be music there—
the ping of each small stone hitting the blade, molecular
vibration, each unspoken thing. If we dig the hole deeper,
what will we hit? Water, ledge-rock, some molten core,
some crack of light, primordial steam. If you've seen this before,
then maybe so have I. There is always a body of water
in my dreams, a leaf-stained reservoir I swim through
with child-limbs and sodden undershirt, panic tendriling
from the bottomless bottom to grab ahold of my foot.
The new studies report that traumatized mice give birth
to fear three generations out. If I tangle the science
to suit the poem, forgive me. Drawing this maze is the only
way I know to spiral myself free. Scribbles and cross-outs.
If a damaged crown is all I can give you, then here it is.

If a damaged crown is all I can give you, then here it is:
our gnarled ligature glistens, splayed. Why do I say *membrane*
when I mean *trauma*? Why do I only say *I miss you*?
What I mean is America is a throat blooming bruise,
an ever-winding sheet. And I am not the only one still
combing an unkempt car, trying to find my misplaced hands
in the ashtray. I am not the only one singing backwards
into an ancestor's grave. The Kaddish makes no mention
of death—just extends itself infinitely, peels our tears from
the earth, uncoils them as blessings into the air. When I say
I'm glad you're not here to witness this, I mean I wish
I knew the difference between mourning and meat.
When I say I keep my rage deep in my teeth, I mean
Grandmother, I'm okay, but the country is not.

I'm okay, but the country is not, says my grandmother
before we follow the music her fingers made. This is how we slip
into memory, how we fall. The final day she succumbs to silence
leaves me a hopeless clot of knuckles and grief. A friend slips
my iron shoes off. Now they're bolted to riverbank cement.
Where have we left our dead? Moraine is a résumé inside
my bones, proof I'll never slip. Smooth as the space we're born to,
we torque the Mobius strip. Our heels sing against the kitchen slate,
blue plates, silverware. Unstring, unstrung. It gives me comfort,
our shared loose tongue. All I wanted was to blossom you back,
but the results come in, one by one, and I've seen this before.
Some will die before spring, some will bloom ragged and yellow.
Bring your shovel. Wherever we go, there'll be music there.
If a damaged crown is all we have, then I'll wear it for you.

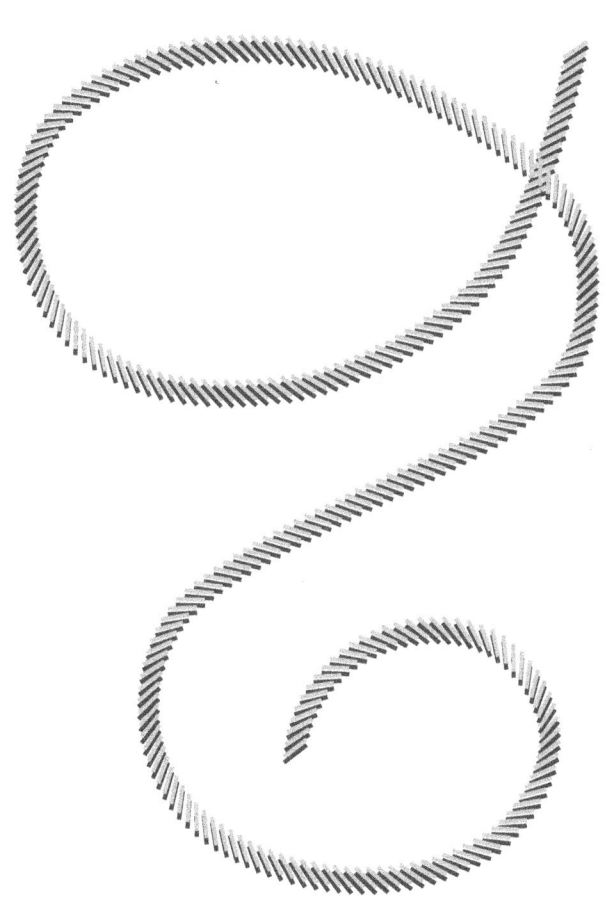

SELF-PORTRAIT AS THE SHADOW, THE VESSEL, AND THE BROKEN HANDLE

Let me cleave with a pencil the way I chop wood, ready for winter—
—F. Douglas Brown

Before my father first turned his two taped-together pencils and bent time
against a newsprint page, he spun his hand in desert sand. High on peyote,
he raised fist to wind, and wind boiled purple into curve and fire. Wind beat wings
and feathered his skin until he glowed a holy vessel. Before I knew madness
burned a wildfire across our family plains, I knew a man hollow as a brass tube
will do anything to fashion himself into a pen and become a conduit
for our darkest dreams. Like ink, we all need someone to bleed.
Even now he rages—toothless, spitting—from the back seat
when I say *believe* as in *he believes he can control time*. He demands you know
he can really do it, that it took great practice, that you have to hold
the pencils just so. He can still squeeze his fist and make us all disappear;
he doesn't deserve this reduction. He only had children
so he could live forever, which is all that anyone wants—
to be the pencils gliding their wingspan across a horizon of endless paper,
to be the whoosh of the axe as it hurls its steel smile ever toward falling,
fleeting moment made infinite as long as you hold it there,
suspended eternally, as long as you ignore what's coming to you, refuse
to reach out and touch the pitted, scarred face of the chopping block.
We all beget our own ends or worse. Call God the father, but no one wants a father
who truly believes he's God. Each autumn I split the wood, maple and ash,
measure my hardness through swing and step. Each frozen morning I lay the fire
in the stove's cold belly then spark a match. I don't love anything I'm not willing
to kill. I won't kill anything I don't love. It took a long time to learn—
I'm still practicing. Each day I grind my body into another day like an axe head

against the bastard file. I'm hungry for the thick thud, the certainty offered
as the arm descends. My father writes from California to say the floodwaters are rising,
the street's a river now, but if he closes his eyes he can pretend it isn't happening.
What's the difference between a child and an executioner? I was born
ready for winter. When I clasp the pencil, I'll draw our eyes open.
When I raise the axe, I'll open my mouth to echo the pitch the blade is singing
and the top of my skull will lift into the sky like a cathedral toward heaven.

My Acupuncturist Tells Me to Have a Conversation with My Pain

Find the center of it, she says, so I tell her
I've learned from poems to climb the fat braid
of my pain like a gym class rope. When she
taps the needles in with the force
of a tiny mallet, I hold my limbs straight
as a chiseled beam, wait for the marionette
strum and pulse, circuit of my body
closing toward itself. I'm high voltage,
charged, she says of the buzzing that courses
my wrists as she brings the needle in close
to my skin—that spring-heeled zapping,
live-wire jolt from finger to toe:
anger through the liver, fear through
bladder and kidneys. She leaves before I can ask
what path grief takes. Alone on the table,
I imagine pain, anger, fear pacing my body
restless—like the skidder roads
I walk each night, rocky ruts that pull
an ankle into itself, twist heel and arch along
the moraine of small stones we've dumped
in the road, tractor load by tractor load
to fill the deepest gaps. *Find the center,*
but it's like trying to locate the volta
of my echoing nightmares, memory fraying
to gray so fast I've already swallowed myself
trying to give it a name. *Pain is my brother,
like the wolf,* quotes my father. This my lineage:
he steals and botches every mythology
until the stories run like spoiled ink
through his veins. He's toxic with suffering—
liquor bottles piled under the desk,

used catheters by the toilet, torment swelling
a lake inside him until you can hear it sloshing
when he walks. This my primary inheritance:
my steadfast refusal to believe that pain
serves no purpose, my hollow leg
for anguish. If I can't carry it in my body
then where will I carry it? And what else
is a body even for? Tendon by fascia by membrane
my body searches for land, my body burrows
a home for itself from the only thing it knows.
Pain, you're that winter rodent cold-clamped and waiting
in the engine of a parked car, your dragged nest
of McDonald's wrappers, dead leaves, some precious
tuft of fur. One day they'll find my father like that,
slumped over his work, spilling into a spell-circle
of glass and week-old bloat. And even then, pain,
yes you—my little sleep-talking teratoma born
of gnash and tooth and scar, of tangle and tailbone—
I'll sweep you through the crawlspace half-heartedly,
chase you to some darker, rootier corner.
I'll fling the salt, light a match, put on a show.
But pain, we both know the game: you'll never leave me,
I'll never banish you. Each week I dust the cobwebs
from the windowsills, leave the spiders unharmed;
each week I watch the spiders rebuild. This our dance
of broken threads, of legs mammocked by the broom—
I tack memorial cards for friends I've lost, solemnly
pin my beloveds' faces to the window trim. Webs
clot with dust, webs silver their brows, weave
sagging crowns. Let rupture make a terrain
of my body, let needles quill a forest of my skin.
Pain, there's no difference between what I fear
and what I love. Animal heart, animal tongue—
here is a place to slumber awhile, and when
you wake hungry, chew off what you need.

STUDY IN EPIGENETIC MEMORY: THE NEUROSIS PERSISTS

To stress the newborn mice, separate them
        from their mother, force her to swim laps

in a small pool three hours a day. The mice
        grow neurotic, no surprise to the scientists,

but when they breed the neurotic mice
        with normal mice, the neurosis persists

three generations out. I search online
        for neurotic behavior patterns in mice

and just get links advising me
        on how to manage my own symptoms

which, WebMD assures me, are caused
        by constant worry and negativity.

Even the internet seems to know
        I'm searching for scorch marks

everywhere, like there's an epicenter,
        a single origin point for the smolder

inside me. Here's my secret about worry:
        I believe most bad things that happen

are things we never think would happen,
        which means each terrible occurrence I conjure

is one less likely to ensue, which is to say I believe
        worrying keeps catastrophe at bay. In my family

A mind that runs a wheel is nothing new.
        Nor is it a sign of captivity-bred neurosis.

Even wild field mice enjoy running
        a metal wheel if one is left out,

and I could free-associate on mice for hours:
        the genetic experiments my husband performed

as a high school intern at a famous lab
        where they once bred a mouse named

Piebald Megacolon who ate and ate
        until he distended with shit and died,

or the mice raised with lesions to test the off-label use
        of the cholesterol drug that might lessen the risk

of bleeding in my sister's brain,
        or the childhood food dish squirming

with babies that time the pet store
        incorrectly sexed our two male mice and sold us

a breeding pair, which is how we discovered
        that once mice start breeding, it's nearly impossible

to contain their population growth. I don't recall
        what we did with the baby mice, probably

sold some back to the pet store
        where they ended up as supper for snakes.

If nothing else, mice are an excellent lesson
        on the vast and tangled histories of human brutality,

which I am considering now, again, reading
        this time about Civil War Confederate soldiers

subjected to starvation in POW camps,
        how their sons were 11% more likely

to die before their peers, an observation
        interrupted by an advertisement suggesting

I might prefer another topic, such as
        What Happens When the Food Runs Out?

or *Wet Countries That Are Running Dry*
        or *Why More Men Take Their Own Lives.*

When the article resumes, it's filled with stock photos
        of families—families prancing along the beach,

families in swimsuits by a tropical lake, families
        arm in arm—the fathers and sons reduced

to shadowed outlines, ghostly hands, bodies replaced
        by bomb-burst and a pulsing, mushrooming fear.

The Thing About Fire

At first the townspeople refused to believe or leave. Then sinkholes began appearing in yards. Now only five residents are left in that Pennsylvania coal town, underground tunnels still smoldering. Because the thing about fire is it starts so quietly at first that you're already breathing the smoke before you smell it. And the thing about fire too is that always somewhere something is burning, and mostly it feels so far away. Until it isn't. California wildfire smoke hazes my Maine skyline until the setting sun dayglows—an orange fester bright as the hens' eggs when we feed them lobster shells. And sometimes fire doesn't have any flames at all. Our apple trees catch a blight and the trunks blacken. Leafy tips wilt and bend. A shepherd's crook, they call it. That inside burning that culls you straight from the flock. We cut one tree down, pull it out roots and all—drag every scoured limb to the bonfire pile, pour gas and torch. The other tree we leave stump protruding awkwardly up, plan to top-graft new scions in spring. Some days it seems everything is built from a scar. Because the thing about fire is sometimes it burns so long the burning itself becomes a form of survival. It becomes the only language we know how to speak. Pines and hemlocks catch me like candlewicks in my sleep. Tips curl, spines collapse. I wake smoldering from the inside, a fever sweat with no fever. I wake with a crackle. I wake contagious into the red throat of it. I could burn myself up with the thoughts in my head. Peel bark back and sing for the stars. Sing for every tiny village crumbling to orange-black rubble inside the hot mouth of the cookstove firebox. Open the firebox and throw another remnant in. Watch ticks pop on the burner plate, a private pyre. Throw in my toenail clippings even. We'll all disappear that fast one day, leave a layer of thick greasy ash behind. Because the thing about fire is it knows what we're after, knows we're already singing its song. Immolation like a hymn in our throats. You want to talk unity? Watch a whole forest ablaze. Watch a canyon breathe itself awake, dragon's breath, our own hot reckoning.

Screw Self-Care

I say to my therapist, and because it's her job to, she tenders,
What if we called it self-compassion instead? On my tongue

compassion is a lotus flower, so thickly petaled,
so unabashedly pink I'll never be sure it's not fake.

Reach out the hand and touch it waxy. If I were a flower
I would pull the petals off myself one by one

simply for the beauty of watching them fall,
but also for the raw naked middle of it—the yellow center,

each ovule waiting to ripen with fruit or seed or—
I promise to be kinder to myself, I say, though I don't yet know

if I mean it. I have tuned myself for the teeth. I have spent
a lifetime practicing. Child in her bedroom pummeling

for beauty, forehead to wall and fist to nose, I blossomed
the font of red amaryllis from my face.

Reach out for the child. I dip my hand in and what
I see on my fingertips when I pull away is bright

with lies. For years I've been walking around quoting
that porno scene—the one where Sasha Grey cries out

and the man fucking her growls back, not unkindly,
It's anal sex, it's supposed to hurt—like it's some kind of mantra

for living. How do we unlearn ourselves? At night I fetal
to the right, body balled until my limbs needle, static me

into sleep. I walk through my dreams in a floral slit evening
gown, carrying a Tupperware, a glass bowl of budding mold

like a strand of black pearls against my chest. What if
I can't distinguish between the burden in me and the gift?

Muscle Memory: A Surgery

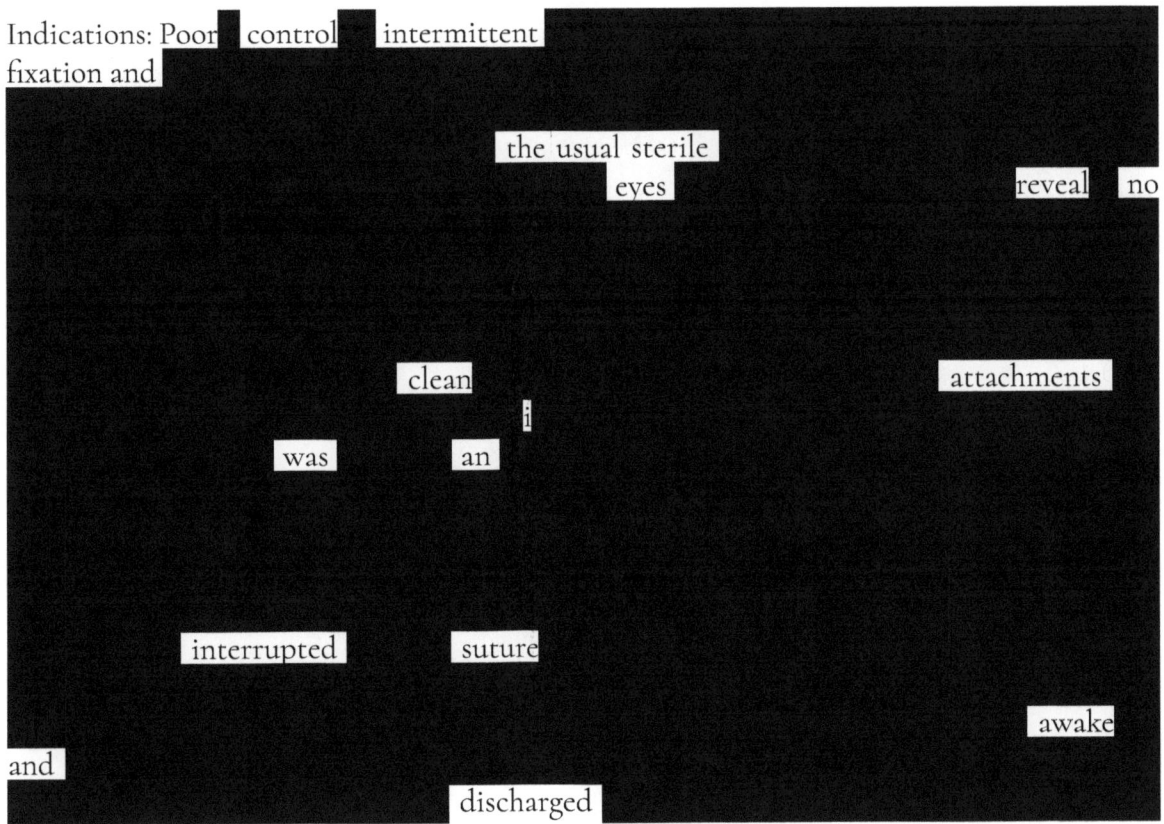

Indications: Poor control intermittent / fixation and / the usual sterile / eyes reveal no / clean attachments / i / was an / interrupted suture / awake / and / discharged

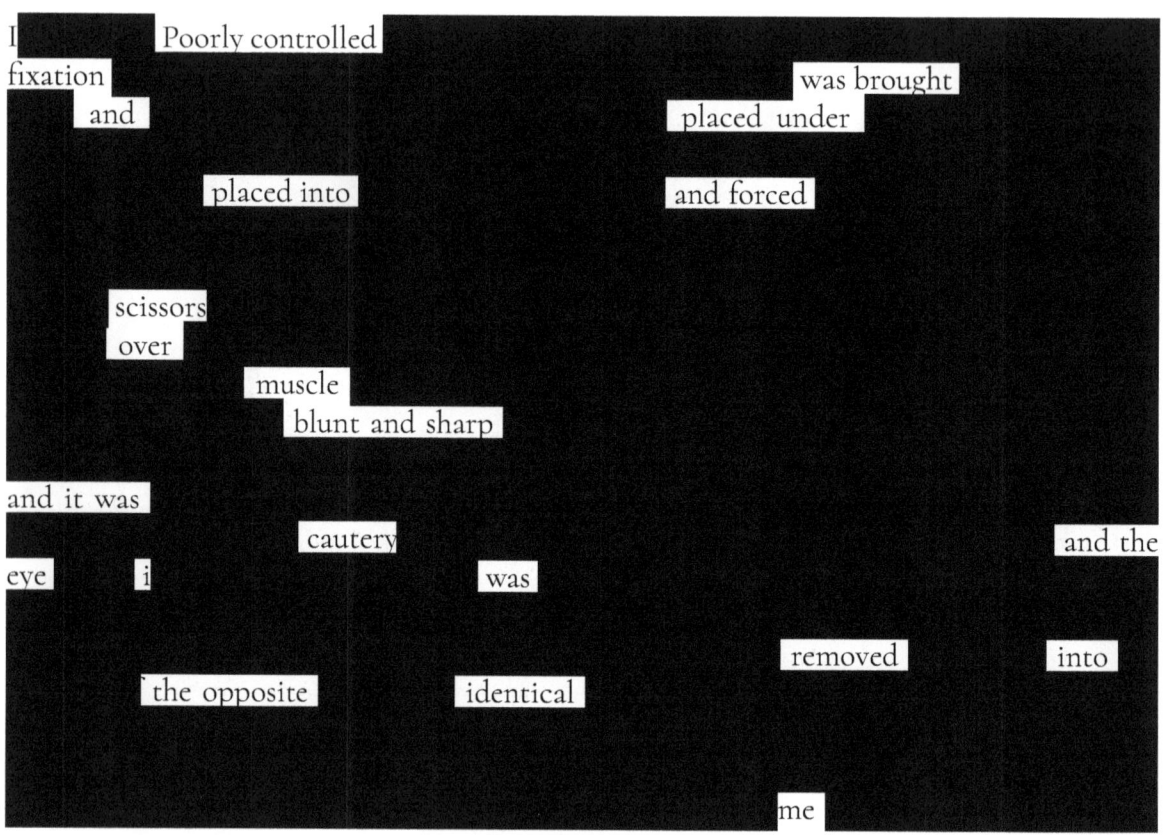

I Poorly controlled / fixation was brought / and placed under / placed into and forced / scissors / over / muscle / blunt and sharp / and it was / cautery and the / eye i was / removed into / the opposite identical / me

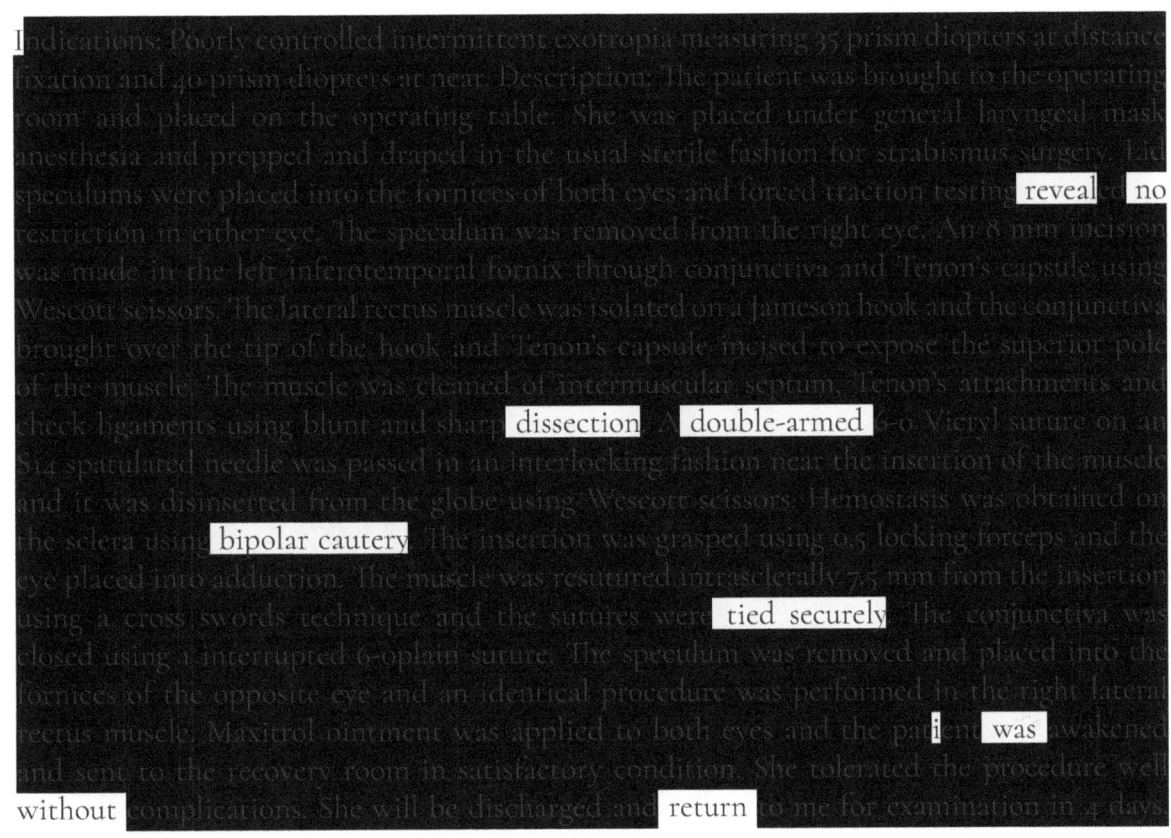

I / reveal no / dissection double-armed / bipolar cautery / tied securely / i was / without return at distance / i was / patient / and tolerated

it / was / and it was / n o t / me

Indications: Poorly controlled **inter**mittent exotropia **me**asuring 35 prism diopters at distance fixation and 40 prism diopters at near. Description: The patient was brought to the operating room and placed on the operating table. She was placed **under** general laryngeal **mask** anesthesia **and** prepped and **drape**d in the usual sterile fashion for strabismus surgery. Lid speculums were placed into the fornices of both eyes and **force**d traction testing revealed no restriction in either eye. The speculum was removed from the right eye. An 8 mm incision was made in the left inferotemporal fornix through conjunctiva and Tenon's capsule using Wescott scissors. The lateral rectus muscle was isolated on a Jameson hook and the conjunctiva brought over the tip of the hook and Tenon's capsule incised to expose the superior pole of the muscle. The muscle was cleaned of intermuscular septum, Tenon's attachments and check ligaments using blunt and sharp **dissection**. A double-armed 6-0 Vicryl suture on an S14 spatulated needle was passed in an interlocking fashion near the insertion of the muscle and it was disinserted **from the** globe using Wescott scissors. Hemostasis was obtained on the sclera using bipolar **cautery.** The insertion was grasped using 0.5 locking forceps and the eye placed into adduction. The muscle was resutured intrasclerally 7.5 mm from the insertion using a cross swords technique and the sutures were tied securely. The conjunctiva was closed using 4 interrupted 6-0 plain suture. **The speculum** was removed and placed into the fornices of the opposite eye and an identical procedure was performed in the right lateral rectus muscle. Maxitrol ointment was applied to both eyes and the patient was awakened and sent to the recovery room in satisfactory condition. She tolerated the procedure well without complications. She **will be** discharged and return to **me** for examination in 4 days.

inter me / under mask / and drape / force / dissection / from the / cautery. / The speculum / will be me

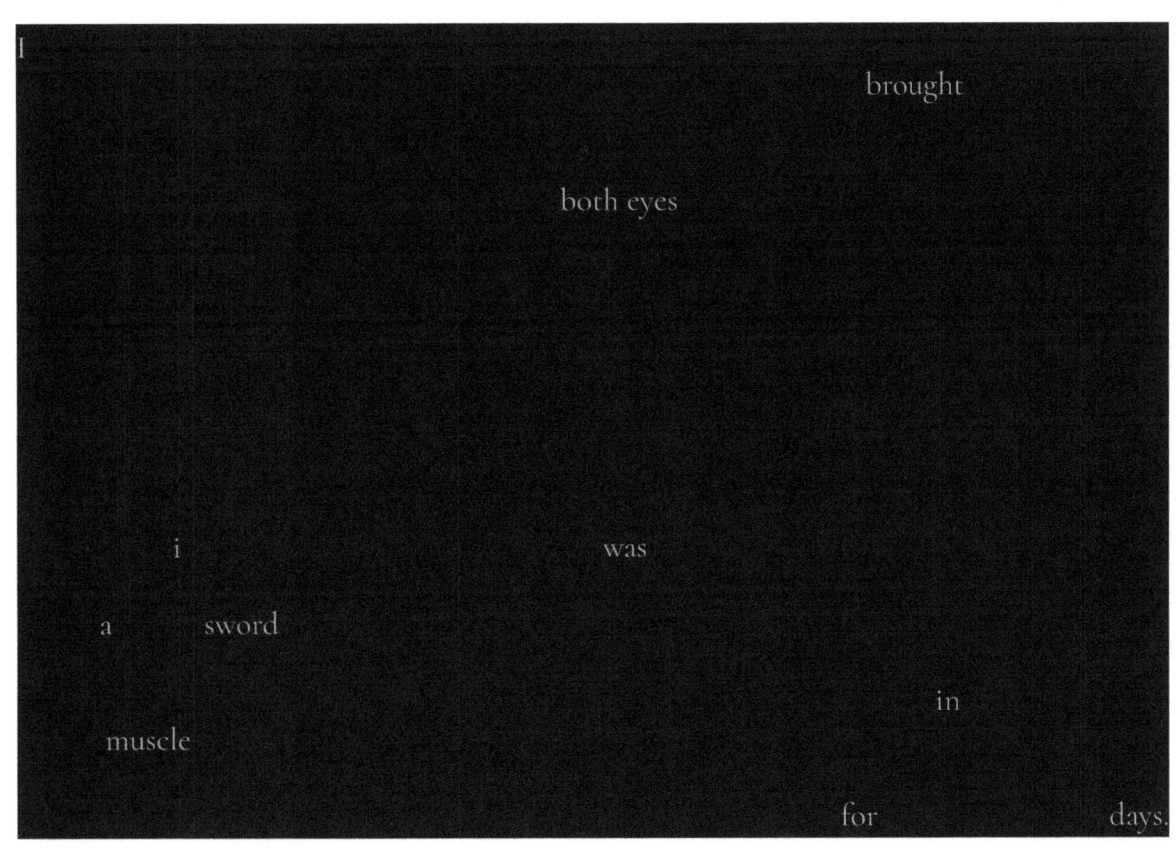

I / brought / both eyes / i was / a sword / in / muscle / for days.

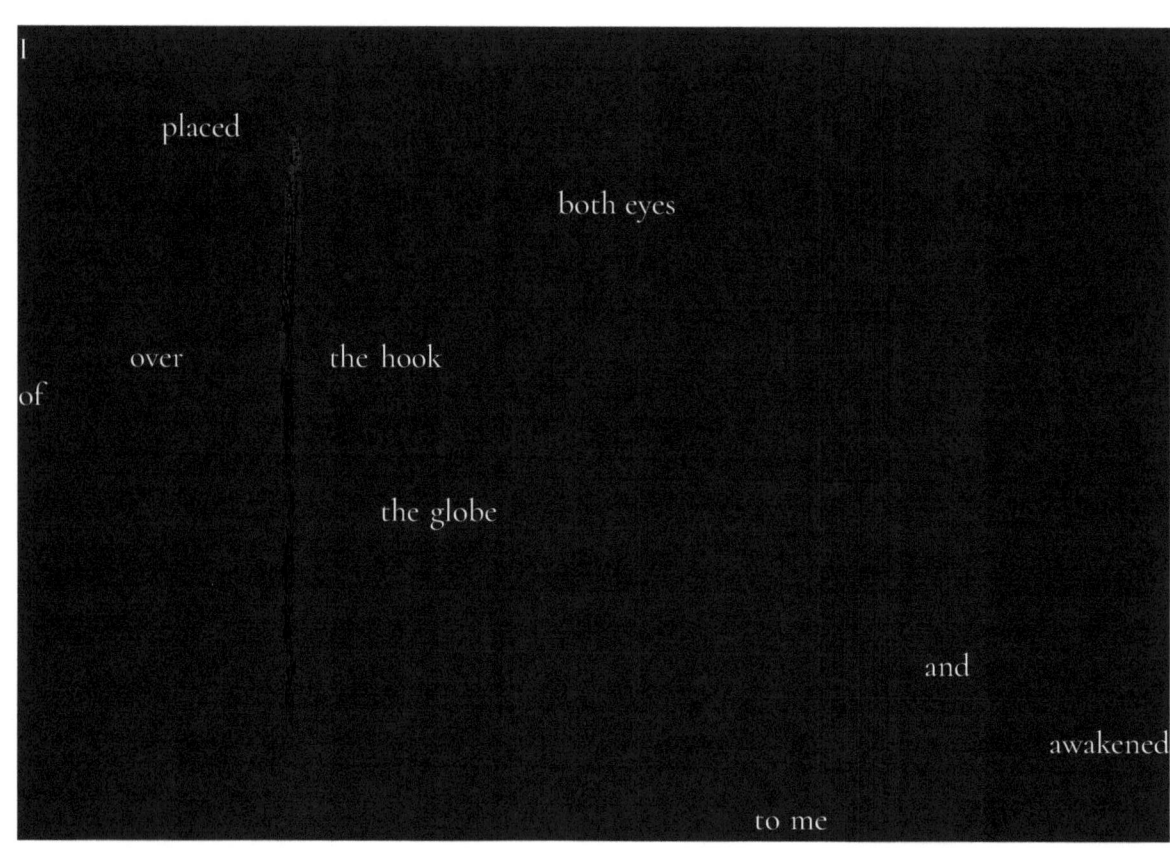

I / placed / both eyes / over the hook / of / the globe / and / awakened / to me

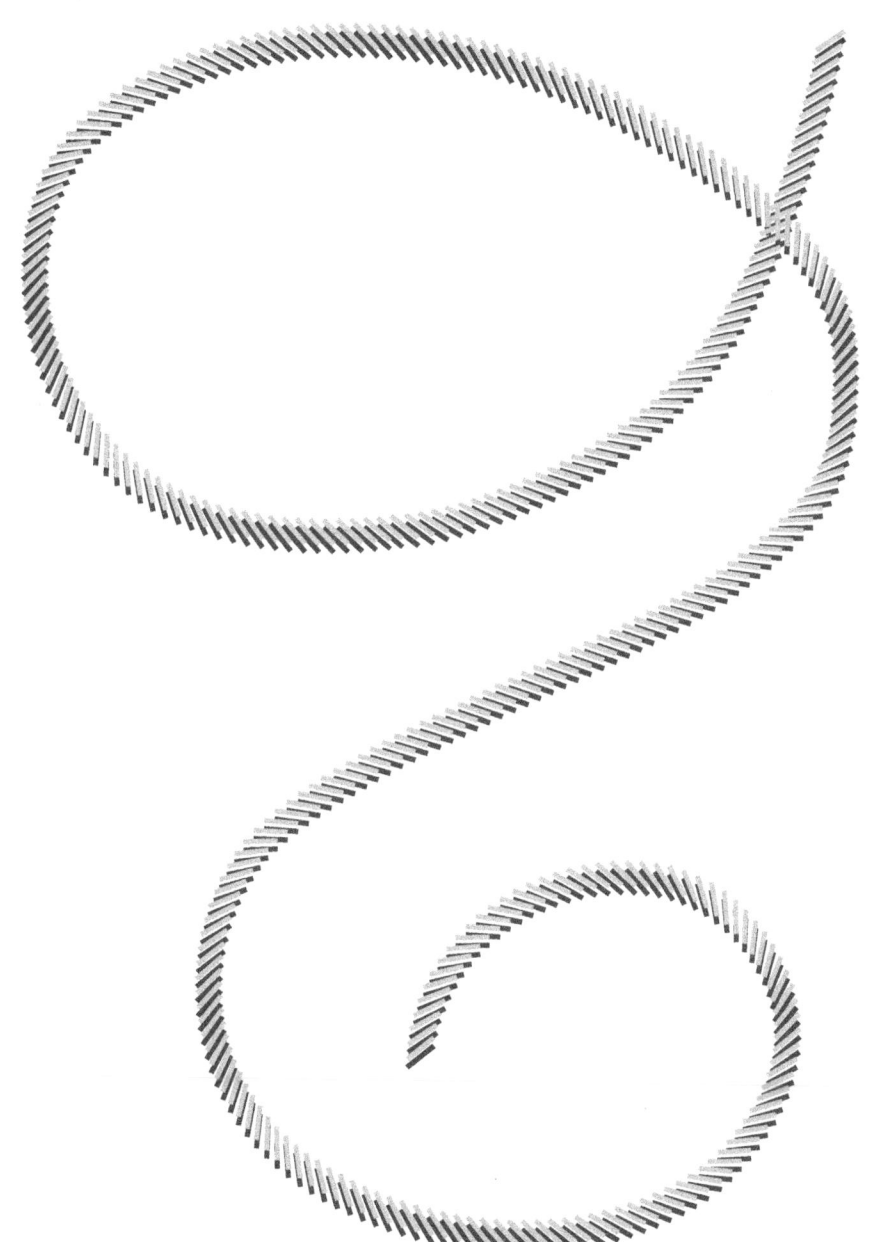

Small-Town Parade / Frozen Lake: Notes on Fear

In the grocery store parking lot I refuse to go inside. Pariah now, I stay door shut in the passenger seat, averting my eyes, hand shielding my face. A man in a mud-crusted jeep stares me down. I don't know him but maybe I know him. It's a week after the parade & everyone's all angry eyes. I'm more seen than I've ever been. I'm less seen than I've ever been. I sit in the parking lot & wait.

Baby, where are you & how long does it take to buy plain yogurt & block ice for the broken refrigerator? I count backward from one hundred, two hundred—until I hear a shopping cart rattle, until I spy your ball cap bobbing across the parking lot as you laugh your loud laugh, as you lean effortlessly into a truck window, as you shoot the shit with a friend & make it look so easy—

I step out onto the frozen lake, wandering the cove beside the slate quarry. The ice is skinned with sleet. My tracks are tangled. I loop a loose figure eight, pass through the hole and back into the needle's eye again and again, layering.

The energy of our bodies sinks when we feel afraid. Something primal is awakened. Animal, we curl inward, protect our vital organs.

The quarry looms behind the lake—a snow-mounded shoulder. It hulks in on itself then gives way without warning, drops sharply into watery pit.

There was a parade in my town. There were floats in the parade. I was in the parade. On the float in front of my float was a brick wall. A boy in a striped prison uniform & blonde wig & the name Clinton slapped on the back of his jumpsuit was bent down on his knees building the wall with mortar & trowel. There was a man dressed as Trump who made the boy build the wall. *Outa Space* said the sign on the float. It was a wordplay. The theme of the parade was supposed to be outer space. The man dressed as Trump gulped a Bud Light from the stash in his wheelbarrow & strutted. I watched it all. It was a hot summer day. He sprayed the boys down with a hose & they hollered for more. One boy almost punched another boy. They were red-faced screaming. The crowd cheered & clapped. The man trumped up their fears & his own too. He danced his own parade. The streets were lined with spectators. Half the town cheered & half the town booed. The float rode right down Main Street & the whole time the sign on the back of the float said: *We all bleed red white & blue.*

Everyone is so afraid they can't decide what to fear most. Everyone is carrying stones. Or maybe only some of us are carrying stones. None of us can decide who is carrying stones.

The town is afraid of change. The town fears what it does not know

The unknown is everywhere. In this town outsiders keep coming, a flood of them. The outsiders love the mountains. The outsiders love the rivers. The outsiders love what they call *this quaint simple way of life*.

The outsiders bring their money. They bring new desires: for expensive goat cheeses, for mountain bikes, for kombucha, for spicy food.

They bring new views, new values. New words. They ask the town to examine itself with a strange new gaze.

And the town, afraid, hunches into itself and hardens like slate.

According to Chinese medicine, fear is the emotion associated with the water element—with the kidneys, with the bladder, and with winter.

Because winter hangs so close to the realm of death, it is the natural season for fear.

Worry knots the Qi, leading to stagnated and circular thinking.

A quarry is both mouth and midden—both the crevasse in which we bury our hearts and the heap of detritus our excavation leaves behind. Its hidden darkness crusts with ice, stone-hard and shining.

In the weeks after the parade I start recalling that summer day a decade & a half ago before this town was ours. We'd followed your sister to a friend's, some guy we didn't know. It was all of us day-drunk, all of us twenty-two, all of us in the sunshine on the front lawn drinking Jim Beam & ginger ale, all of us smoking Camels or American Spirits, all of us young, our love so young, so careless. We were all of us joking about this & that, saying who was *from here* & who was *from away*. I was from away & you were from here & someone said *Masshole* & I said, *What's that, I'm not that*. You were smiling as you took my hand, as you took a drag of your cigarette. You were smiling & the sun was shining. It was midsummer & the town not yet ours. We were drinking whiskey, we were twenty-two & you were smiling as you said, *No, we have another word for you.*

The pericardium is the sac. Around the heart. It absorbs all pain. To protect the heart.
It sets the tone. Of contraction and tension. Within our bodies. We each build
our own rhythms. We each ossify. Our own armor. When we feel afraid.
Shoulders roll. And shrink.

Fear comes when we are faced with the unknown with change with a shifting surface
with cavern with the threat we will break—

the ice expands as it thickens, leading to stress fractures and sudden
popping sounds. Gunshots under our feet. The ice triggers
our fear response even as it hardens beneath—

We call our neighbor *the gatekeeper*, and it's a joke, but it's also not. Her house is the first one on this hill as you come up the road and she's got way more and bigger guns than us. We call this hill where we live an *easily defensible hill*, which is also a joke but not: this question of what we'll all do when the proverbial or literal shit ever hits the fan. Our neighbor has boxes of freeze-dried oatmeal and space-blankets and bandages and cases of cans of Chef Boyardee and 120 rolls of toilet paper the last time she counted. She says anyone not prepping is just being stupid, that she sure as shit won't be left with her pants down. Us, we don't call ourselves anything, but it's true there are rows of canning jars laid up in our cellar and a stash of old antibiotics under the kitchen sink. All our friends say this is where they'll go if they can make it out of the cities alive. Our neighbor says no, they can't come unless they have a skill, and I argue with her. I want to fight for everyone worth saving, which I think is most all of us. So we spend the evening with our neighbors, laughing and quarreling about it over beers and the line between surreal and real keeps pressing closer—like when you overstuff a jar of dilly beans before you lower it into the boiling water. Then the bottom pops out and it shoots glass, brine, and beans all through your canning pot.

On a frozen lake at snowfall, everything is whiter, wider, further, closer than it seems—

my vision inflates and constricts.

Always I have followed language like the snowmobile trail that cuts across this frozen lake.

The ice pops loudest close to the quarry.

The black slate beneath and beside this lake is famous and highly prized for tombstones.

In the old photographs the open-pit slate mines gape like Tartarus. The cut ledges lend a grave-like air. A staggering fall. Workers stepped into the box and were lowered into the pit by a hoist. The slate was brought up to the top of the quarry by the same chains used to lower the box.

If there is anything that would surely provoke fear it is being lowered by chains into a pit shaped like a grave.

All I did was write a letter I believed language was a raft believed our mouths were all our ocean after the parade I wrote a letter passed the letter around a reporter called I spoke to the reporter no one else would I wasn't born in this town I wasn't but I thought I was a part when word got out they said *you will never be from here now* word got out & all the words ran together all the words ran together

& all the words ran together all the words ran together & all the words ran together all the words ran together & all the words ran together all the words ran together & all the words ran together all the words ran together & all the words ran together all the words ran together & all the words ran together

It is not impossible that you might fall into your own worst moment and remain preserved there forever.

Once, a doe and her fawn tumbled into the pit mine. Their bodies lay where they fell. It was clear they died on impact. When the photographer saw them he photographed their corpses, their bones. The photograph is in a museum now.

In the maw of the quarry, one sees nothing but walls of shiny black stone—a panopticon of reflective darkness, the self mirrored back to itself. You can't avoid breathing in your own fear, lungfuls of falling.

When I read the comments after writing the letter, I felt a sinking inside me, an ice-built ship.

When I listened to the tape of the town meeting, listened to the accusations against me, my heart became the lake, constricting and expanding and constricting again.

What I fear most is not being invisible but being seen and misunderstood.

When I listened to the tape of the selectman's meeting after holding the file for months unable to listen,

when I finally listened, my heart began

to thump &
pulse inside my chest

harder with each beat the way ice
c r a c k s   a s   i t   e x p a n d s   m y   p a l m s   w e n t   t o   f i s t s

sweaty clench I listened & the ice cracked inside

Later I told my friend who was writing a play on the Salem witch trials told him I was afraid & what I felt was fear.
of my fear I ashamed I felt was fear.
of my fear & afraid of
me & my shame was fear.
Of course he replied
me & what I because each of us
me & what I felt was there's a kernel of
me & what I felt was fear. doubt that really deep
down what
me & what I felt was fear. they're say-
ing about us
that really
me & what I felt was fear. it might
be true

The night after I listened to the tape for the first time
              I dreamed I was at a party with my accusers.

          They were laughingdrinkingtalking
        smack. I stood among them, watched,
       even laughed a little at my own expense.

            They didn't recognize me.

     I kept wondering when they would recognize me and what
              they would do when they did.

When I awoke it was suddenly and with the fear I was crushing
a small creature with my body—

          something writhing and squeaking
          between my back and the bedsheet.

Still I was careful I spoke in questions I was raised to believe that questions are a form of love & so I was so careful so careful said *we* when everyone else said *us* or *them*

I was so careful I actually believed if I were careful enough my words might matter— what I said or did not say—but

everyone already knew was so sure they already knew what I'd meant to say.
everyone already knew was so sure they already knew what I'd meant to say.

The question that lingers is did I betray language or did language betray me?

Because the words kept splintering—they bounced off themselves, refracting—and I was taught to follow language like the trail that slices the frozen lake.

But what if the trails all lead back to the lake's center?

The only thing I would not give was

                        my silence.
                        My silence

                                              was the only thing wanted
                                              from me.

The knot at the nape of my neck where my shoulders hump corresponds to the thickness at my throat called goiter which corresponds to the fissure of small cracks in the lining of my bladder which corresponds to my fear.

A woman's kidney energy is complete by the age of seven. As my acupuncturist places the needles she says, *Fear in childhood, a sense of instability*. She says, *Picture a chimney with missing bricks*. She says, *This is your body*.

Which is to say that as I squat to release burning piss on the frozen lake I am attempting to rid myself of fear.

Underneath my feet I know a cold writhing lies in wait, the slow bodies of togue, brook trout, salmon twining the slate outcrops.

Set the foot down with distrust on the crust of the world—it is thin, warns Edna St. Vincent Millay.

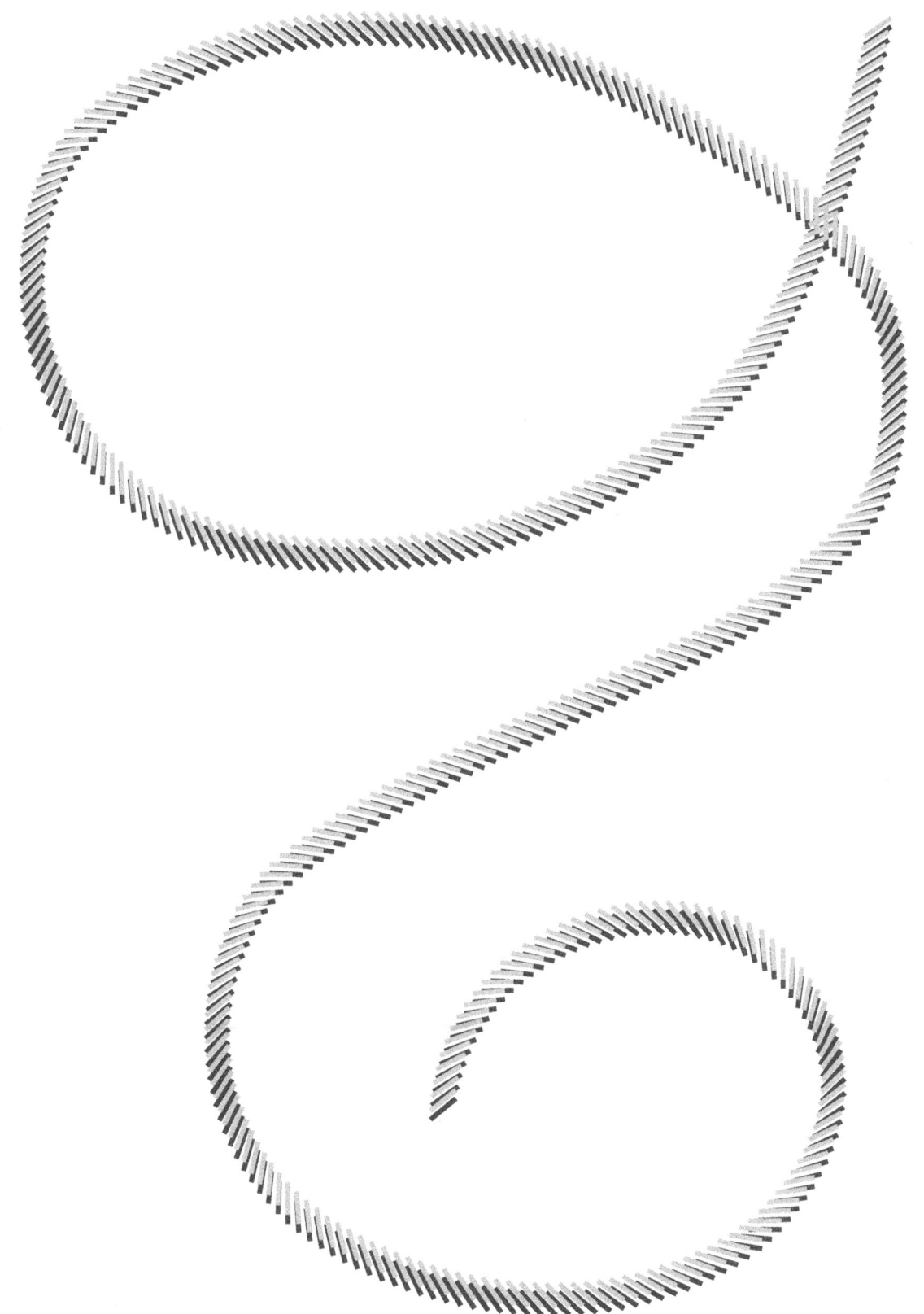

Drought Diary

When I wake my belly is full with impending rain, forehead furrowed to cloud. A mess, I go to write on my neighbors' porch. My neighbors are never there, so I shit in their outhouse, leave the door open and stare at their orchard. All the leaves are yellow. All the leaves are orange. All the leaves are fallen brown and damp with almost rain. When my shit falls into the hole, it makes a heavy thud like an animal approaching, one footfall at a time. The past animal tense of *shit* is *shat*. I close the door, walk down into the orchard, steal an apple. The apple is red, Snow-White shiny, but the flesh inside is stippled worm. I eat the worm. I eat the blight. Rain begins to fall on my keyboard. Mornings like this, words juice out my mouth. It has been a long summer of not enough rain. *Sault* is a fall in a river. It has been a long fall of not enough rain. The river is now a ravel of bones, all her drops exposed and gaping. *There is no ecologically safe way to mourn,* writes Diana Khoi Nguyen. sigh. Deer ticks collect in my toward the heat. Each day I until they rut me up—pronate chiropractor says I'm beginning I read that melancholy is a mourning for myself or for all hard to find when it's dry like on water I have to remember is all edges these days. If I slip If I fall with the river, I fall as become an *assault*. If the drop is upon myself. When I turn the and sputters with pocketed silt drift down. The Al-Anon which it says is not the same as rage, it says, go to the garden, *Sault* pronounced *so*—a deep hair then travel surreptitiously walk these old skidder roads or supinate my steps. The to twist to the right. Yesterday mourning for the self. Am I of us. The parameters are too this, dry this long. We're so low not to wash my hands. The river on the rocks, I fall into the river. the river. If I fall as the river, I in my heart, then the assault is tap, the water pours silt, hisses air. Fill a bucket and let the handbook praises detachment, bottling one's rage. To remedy pull weeds and imagine you are ripping out the alcoholic's hair. Dig and imagine you are digging his grave. Some of the things I have dug holes for include dead dogs, fruit trees, outhouses, flowers that wilted for lack of watering. Things my ancestors have dug holes for may or may not have included themselves. Once I pierced a toad with my pitchfork while digging potatoes. I didn't know what to do with the toad or my shame, so I simply mounded the dirt back up and left it. The last time the well ran dry I watched my husband dig but did not step down in to help. Usually digging is a solitary act—there's no room for someone else inside a hole. When I take a bite of apple and see half a worm, I think, *What if all my walls were made of flesh?* A poem could rightly be called a hole. I write until I cannot feel my fingertips. Rain stipples the keyboard. Inside me is a dark well waiting for rain. Inside me is all of us waiting, darkly, for rain. The waterline hovers—just above the foot valve.

I Have No Answer but Stones

Who will walk / Between me and the crying of the frogs?
—Edna St. Vincent Millay

Either you believe, or you don't, my friend says. *Which is it?*
We're parked on the dirt road in darkness, beer bottles balanced

on the hood of her truck. It's Passover, and I'm speaking in stories again,
counting them out like drops of wine on a white serving plate:

one for blood, two for frogs. In the bog below the hill the peepers
weave a net of their shrieking; they cinch the night's throat taut.

How to say I believe most in the power of what I do not know,
secondly in the power of that which I can hold in a closed fist?

We collect stones from the road by headlamp. My friend likes
purple ones best. This is how I learned to carry stories, to tuck them

into my pocket, familiar weight chafing my thigh—
what my ancestors must have carried, shuffling toward exile.

A story pressed onto a child's tongue is not the same as bread,
but it will suffice for a time. *Before me a woman bends under her bundle.*

From the bundle a thin string of rice keeps pouring over the street...
I think of nothing, wrote fourteen-year-old Yitzchak Rudashevski in his diary

the day Vilna Jews were herded to the ghetto. What does one haul with
a body that doesn't know its own ghosts? If the stories clink like stones

at the bottom of my empty sack, they give me a rhythm to walk by.
If they rattle bones or doorknobs on nights as dark as this one,

I know I'll let them in. *Listen,* I tell my friend, then stop.
I have no answer. I drink more beer. I load my pockets with more

and larger stones. Each year the frogs shrill a tower of glass
to the top of the sky. Each year they scream until it shatters us.

A Catalog of Endlings

Aurochs, in 1627, in what's now Poland—their pre-bovine bodies found
in a forest, not far from killing fields where my own ancestors might be.

Benjamin in 1936, the last Tasmanian tiger, of neglect, pacing her cage
at Hobart Zoo. And don't forget Booming Ben, solitary heath hen.

Celia the Pyrenean ibex. They tried to clone her back from extinction
and, for seven minutes, she was not the last; but her clone couldn't breathe.

Dusky seaside sparrow: the one called Orange Band, held captive
at Discovery Island, Disney World.

Every extant being, each of us, eventually, extinct.

Fatu, daughter of Najin, last of the northern white rhinoceros.

Golden toad last seen in 1989. George the Oahu tree snail.

Hurricane Dorian took the last Bahama nuthatches, or so they suspect.

I have no children, nor does my sister. Thus ends our branch
of the family tree. I offer my mother no shelter from this grief.

Julia, the bald ibis, shot down mid-migration.

Kauaʻi ʻōʻō last seen in 1985, last heard in '87.

Lonesome George, the Pinta Island tortoise, lived to 102.
At the end, magazines called him the rarest creature in the world.

Martha, last passenger pigeon, was named for Martha Washington, strange joke
of history, her remains now housed in a steel Smithsonian storage locker.

Nobody knew or cared when the endlings died, writes Eric Freedman, who coined the term. *It is deep-to-the-bone chilling to know the exact date a species disappeared...*

Organs are removed in taxidermy. Martha's live in a jar of embalming fluid, the rest of her wired to branch and Styrofoam, beside a male she never knew.

Po'ouli birds gone too. None seen in nearly twenty years.

Quagga dead 250 years, killed for meat and skins.

Rufous-fronted laughingthrush—just one left now, in Java.

Surviving specimen, last of its species. How simple it is to just disappear. Sentimentality won't save any of us in the end.

Tarpan, 1909, in captivity. Toughie the Rabb's fringe-limbed tree-frog. Turgi the last Polynesian tree snail.

Unnoticed mostly.

Various causes.

Women's hats wanted bright tail feathers. It was that plus deforestation that took the Carolina parakeet.

X is the loudest letter in *extinction*. X marks the spot. *It is even more ghastly to look upon the place where it happened and know...*

Yangtze giant softshell turtles are down to only three.

Zoo plaque, museum box: the lucky ones. Most gone before we name them—our caring only born to shape in absence.

Home Movie with Storm, Orchard, and News

Snow to rain to sleet. I peel clementines, drop my rinds to the firebox.
All the trees in our orchard are ice-glazed, glassy with threat of breaking.
It's called a ghost apple: the fruit rots out, a husk of ice remains in its shape.

—

All the trees in our orchard are glazed and glassy with threat of breaking.
When the fruit rots out, a husk of ice remains. Call it ghost apple—
an ice-bound absence. Memory without flesh or sweet still holds its shape.

—

When the fruit rots out, a husk of ice remains. Call it ghost apple:
without flesh or sweet, memory shapes an ice-bound absence.
I play the video again, watch the endless gray horizons racing by.

—

Without flesh or sweet, memory shapes an ice-bound absence—
I press play: endless gray horizons race by on the video again,
a 1928 reel marking my great-grandfather's visit home to Mažeikiai.

—

I press play to let endless gray horizons race by again. The video
reel of my great-grandfather's 1928 visit home to Mažeikiai is marked
with cracks, black smudges over house, orchard, his brothers, their families

—

My great-grandfather's 1928 visit home to Mažeikiai is a marked reel
that cracks black smudges over houses and orchards, his brothers, family,
a home he never saw again. Perished, murdered. Already, he'd changed his name.

—

Now in Gaza black smudges crack over houses, orchards, brothers, families
who'll never see home again. Perished, murdered. Grief changes a name
or swallows it whole. History erases and repeats us like a cracked reel—

—

who never sees home again? Who perished, murdered? Grief changes our names,
swallows us. History erases any whole, repeats, repeats like a cracked reel—
the line for flour where even food falls like bombs, bloodied car, child hiding.

—

History swallows history whole, erases any—. Repeats us until the reel cracks,
falling like bomb blasts on a flour line, on a child hiding in a bloodied car,
each day a terrible new list. It does not stop. I found my ancestors' names

—

and it felt like falling. Bloodied blast of a child hiding in a car, in a flour line,
each new day. I found my ancestors' names on a terrible list. It will not stop. I list
toward language, prayerless though I am, threaded by a tangle of silence.

—

Ancestors, how to stop these terrible lists? Each day a new name not found.
Thread us toward language, prayerless and tangled by silence though we are,
where home's song rings endless—*never again, never never never*—for all.

Dream with Jericho Brown, Peaches, and Grief

Hardest self pressed against tenderest self, I was a child but not.
In the dream everything was thick as yellow layer cake with peaches.

Yellow layer cake thickened my dreams: peaches, burnt sugar.
I'd fallen asleep. My love, packed dense with grief, lay in my arms.

My love grieved. Dense snow outside, the packing kind. My arm fell
asleep. I woke: In an airport. On a sidewalk. Next to Jericho Brown.

Jericho Brown woke me up on a sidewalk. I'd fallen through air,
landed flat, my ears ringing. Like one of his duplexes, he said.

Once my love and I shared a duplex. On the landing I flattened my ear
to the wall to hear the fighting of strangers on the other side.

Sometimes I am a wall, a stranger fighting myself on the other side.
My love's brother was dying. I held him. Our fear sweat the bedsheet.

I held my love. No antidote for the sweat and bedsheet of a dying brother.
We were not children. Our hardest selves pressed us tender as we slept.

WHAT WILL YOU DO AT THE END OF THE WORLD?

When I watch the video where the violinist plays
as surgeons cut the cancer from her brain,
my first impulse is to descend into metaphor—
to imagine the plaintive cry of her violin as a singular
silvery thread that leads the surgeons—sublimely,
tremulously—through the Minotaur's maze,
so they can extract the tumor abutting the lobe
that controls her left hand, so they can navigate
the fleshy labyrinthine folds and electric shocks
that make a human mind. When I watch her bow
graze the ventilator tube again and again,
I recollect the old story of Nero playing
as Rome burned, which is supposed to be a story
about callous cruelty and ineffectual leadership,
but which fails to hold up under historic scrutiny
for many reasons, including that the violin
was not invented until the 11th century.
Still, the fable lends him more humanity than not—
the notion that there was music inside him,
even if it took six days of burning to fan it out,
a music so powerful it forced itself to escape
his tyrant's mouth. If art is only pleasure,
Nero's act is selfish, loathsome, but if art is survival—
a violin's siren might morph to beacon
against the smoky air. I keep asking my poems
what the world needs from me in these days
of quickening dread, of burgeoning conflagration,
what they want me to do. In the comments section
below the hospital video, no one can agree
on what they're seeing: *Creepy, incredible,
horrifying, beautiful.* Afterward, the violinist recalls,
I kept thinking, Get out of my way. I need to play louder.

The Book on Self-Compassion

says the literal meaning of compassion is "to suffer *with*." Leave out
the *with*, and I must suffer my own company, alone. Some days
I am a room with no door. I roam the perimeter. I tongue
the keyhole into a poem. But I do not leave. *It is a terrible thing
to be left alone with one's thoughts*, says my husband after I return
from a trip. I cut a hole inside a hole and call it a *house*. I house
my suffering there. *Poets like verbing their nouns*, I explain to a man
at the library when he asks why I speak so strangely. In my dreams
a boil erupts on my shoulder and a host of skinny worms
streams out. *Never will I show mercy to myself*, I once wrote in a poem.
Too often, my regret surfaces as an urge to bite my own hands.
Some days I scroll the screen aimlessly, looking for entry, searching
for the infestation. Computerized images of neurotransmitters erupt
galaxies before my eyes—noded bioluminescent worms, forests
of tendriling dendrites, jellyfish cities of light, a star that swims
like an octopus conjoined to the arms of another. Inside us
Milky Way explosions burst buckshot across these mirroring rifts
we all of us call sky. The wounds light up like cancer under the dye.
Each wound with a neon sign flashing *open*. The verb in me hums,
an ungrounded wire. Maybe, just maybe, it's not the spark
but the darkness between that maps us back.

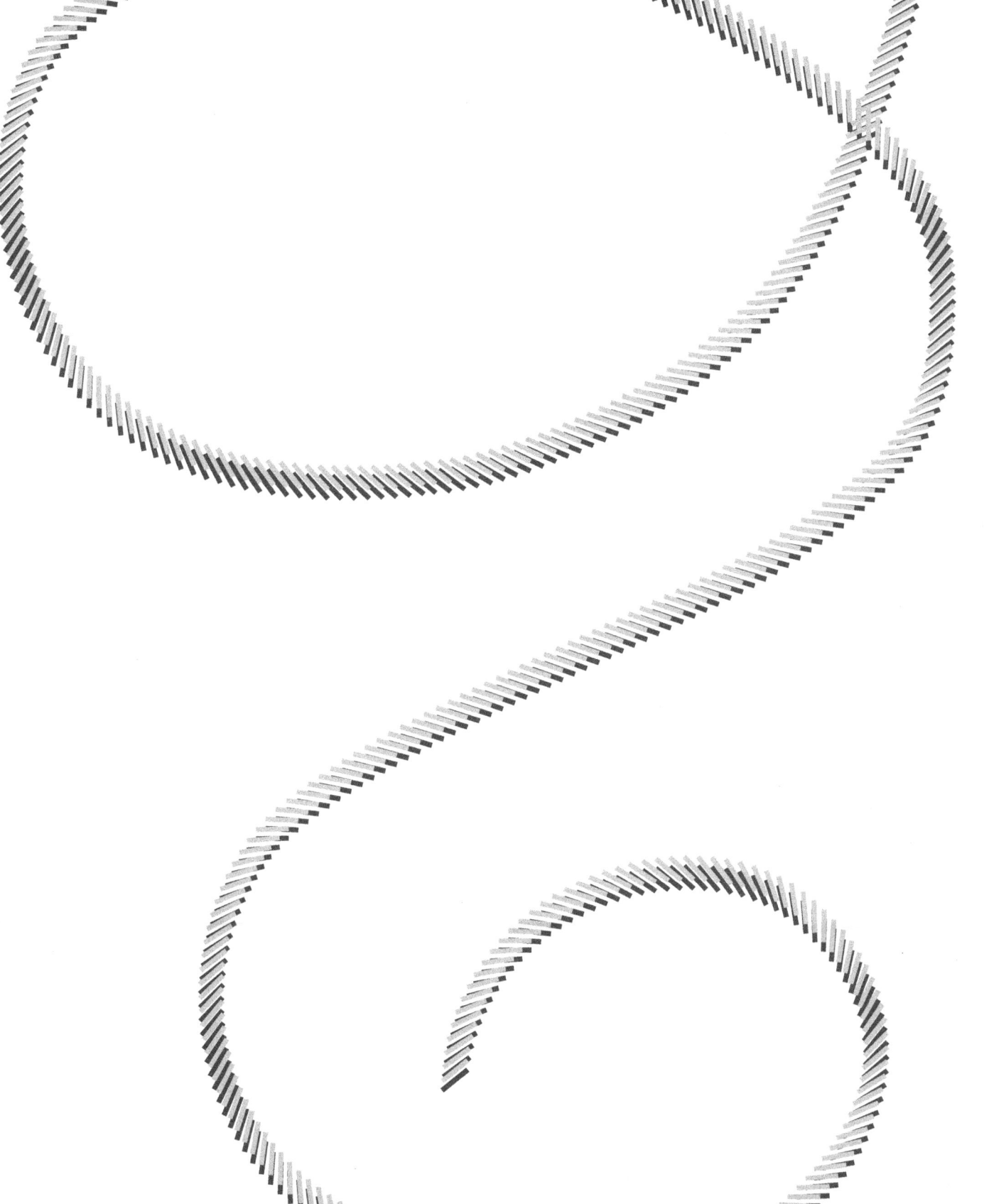

To a Mainer Living 100 Years from Now

The other day I stood beneath an ash tree as old as the time
between my writing this letter and you reading it.

Inside the green moment of the forest, I traced my finger
across the ash's trunk, grooved bark staggered like vertebrae,

a deer bent back to listen, quiet flanks reddening the stillness
before crouch became bolt and it leapt into a lattice

of blackberry cane and brush. Tell me, unknown friend,
what has dissipated from our home and what remains?

Does it still snow hard enough to swallow your footsteps in light?
Do you drink sap each spring, boil your sorrow into new waft and gold?

We lived here at the edge of the old rituals, lived there
until we could not discern our hope from our fear—

wildfire smoke smeared a low brow of bruise, a language written
in billowing keloids and contrails, vanishing welts of vapor.

Are you still repeating our same old violences or have you learned
new ones? Can you wring a chicken's neck with your hands—twist

and pull the throat in unison as my grandmother's grandmother
did and I do now? Or have you colonized Mars, erected skyscrapers

of cosmic concrete? Scientists are at it now, discovering a building material
of human tears, sweat, urine, blood. It hardens fast and cheap, stronger,

they say, than anything we've ever known before. For you I wish nothing
but birdsong. I wish you a pond of peepers screaming spring thaw.

And all those apple trees I planted—it's early autumn now,
their striated skins seeping blush into white flesh as they ripen—

do they still stand on this hill? Pick one for me, please, if they do.
Bite down among stippled wormholes and taste our blinding sweetness.

Further Notes on Fear

When it finally found us, our village was already
a hunched shoulder, had already shouldered our fear

for so long it now shouldered us—fear stitched
our topography, molded hilltops and quarry ledges of us,

our backs ossifying beneath mud-shifting ground,
caking earth, our roots morphed to granite or slate,

bouldered as we were to each new threat, unable
any longer to differentiate. Stone-jawed,

we donned white swaths to obscure
our mouths from neighbors, or our neighbors

from our mouths. We were all open maw behind
our carapaces. We scoffed at those who *live in fear*,

grimaced our grocery carts too closely down aisles.
We did not know if what we feared was already

inside us. We knew how to fight. We did not
know how to fight such invisible terror, so we

purchased more guns, more ammo, we clamored,
we washed or refused to wash, sealed ourselves

inside our homes. We did not stay home. The children
were not in school. We didn't know the difference.

We tallied up license plates from out of state,
baptized doorknobs with isopropyl. Deflated

ditch flowers of latex gloves. Trees in the road,
blockades to keep those from the cities out. Or keep

them in. We didn't know, and so what spread
through us was like the thawing river's rage

at first collapse—we snow-churned, we runneled,
we deluged with debris. One stone dislodged

and then another. We spilled and spilled, clotted leaves
in the dam. Nightly we shipwrecked ourselves,

knotted our loved ones to the mast
with our tongues, sang our old siren's song:

*Glory is our dread for it shall bind us
to our work.* We knew work. Yes, we knew

how to work, but we no longer had jobs
so made lists of tasks we could not complete:

baked, built, swarmed, drank from stale taps,
planned and tilled victory gardens,

quibbled the numbers, proclaimed each
new measure a tyranny. Our waiting

became a tyranny. Each day we
prepared for the Once and for All

and each day the Once and for All
never came—just another low long wave

of panic gathering itself, an icy roiling
wall of building water—until

there was nothing left. Nothing
we could think of to do. We stared

at our hands. How detached.
they appeared. They looked inside out:

muscle, nerve, tendon, artery—each red-
purple, moon-pale tributary—all of us

glistening an unearthly light,
suddenly unsheathed to the bone.

BEAUTY STANDARDS HAVE FALLEN UNDER LOCKDOWN

On Monday I want to dye my hair silver, shave it asymmetric
from right ear to the base of my neck. When I tell Walker
he recoils. I leave the hair dye in my online shopping cart until
it sells out. We get drunk and eat a whole blueberry pie
with a charred top crust and a raw bottom crust, sugar missing
from the middle. He goes to bed early, snores with the dog
through a haze of beer breath. I rise at 5:30, do a yoga video,
make muffins with four kinds of fruit. On the sunny mornings
I ugly cry for hours, but on rainy ones I'm resolute, resigned.
Walker says he's fed up with my sadness, calls me selfish, a drain.
We fight until he reads to me about murder hornets in Washington,
big as your thumb, one sting enough to kill a large man. I am sad
every spring, but this spring there is nowhere for my sorrow to go.
The dog pisses in the corner again. This whole house stinks.
I ball laundry into the washer, sweep the floor into a storm
of dust and fur. When I scroll social media at 3 am, comments
rage about government overreach, invoke the boxcars
my ancestors did not escape, call the governor Führer.
In high school I used to steal Nazi biographies from the back
of the library, horde razorblades under my mattress. The world's
job is to leave us scarred. I am ashamed of the words I have yelled
at Walker during a fight. I am ashamed of the things I have carved
into my skin, grateful for any keloid that fades with time. The poet's
job is to keep seeking out pain, to force some beauty from all
this mess, to hold the hornet up to the candle flame and watch
the world through its burning wing. Sing the poison out, love,
I am hot for the sore. Out on the porch, we inhale the soft after-edge
of rain, extend our fingers into dusk. At the tree line the bobolink
drops a wine glass from its throat and then another. Listen
to our falling shards—this synchronous, translucent breaking.

What's Efflorescing We've Been Afraid to Say

I have been distracted thinking about rotten fruit: oranges, grapefruits, what is withering in yellow decay at the bottom of my refrigerator, what is the size of the blood clot that fell from my mother the day after she bore me. What is shame. What is things we don't write about for 600. On the table the tulips are opening obscenely, splaying their purple darkness. Last week all nineteen of my hens were torn at the throat, left for dead. I gathered them in grain sacks, hauled them far into the trees. I let my sentiment make a waste of good meat. My mother says forceps bruised my infant skull into a banana for two whole weeks. She tells me not to write her into anymore poems. Sometimes she confuses my poems for knives. When I stabbed the injured hen again and again in the head, it was as an act of mercy. Blood pulsed and smeared my palms. I scrubbed the heat and stick with snow. What wounds our ministrations make. I wish to write my mother a poem she won't distrust, a poem that owns the blood but blossoms her heart, tulips her heart, hyacinths her heart. Daffodils its chambers into an entire hillside of spring. Like how she says she forgives the botched stiches. It was worth it, she says, to hold me: I smelled so sweet in elevators other women mistook me for a bouquet.

STUDY IN EPIGENETIC MEMORY: FLOWER AND PETAL

Researchers spray the scent of cherry blossoms
      while administering electric shocks to the feet of male mice
           in order to trace the bow of the mind's sticks and shoots—

how trauma twists our DNA. Once the mice learn the smell
      of pink tumbling only as pain, they are bred, their pups
           fostered out to mice who've never encountered

such honeyed deceit, but when the cherry blossom odor
      is released into the air, the young show alarm, grow jumpy
           and nervous. These offspring of perfumed damage,

of bright spring weeping—their bodies remember, their bodies
      distrust. The fear fades in second and third generations,
           yet lingers on. A *sensitivity,* the researchers say.

Most of the flowering cherries sold in stores are abominations,
      weeping Higan limbs top-grafted to a straight cherry trunk.
           An ornamental cherry lives no more than forty years.

When the researchers dissect the mice, they discover,
      in the small buds of their brains, a greater number
           of neurons able to detect the cherry scent.

But still, we know little—just the small cruelties of fact: they sugar
      and helix and drift, graze contorted branches, our outstretched
           fingertips, as memory drops its petals all around us.

Elegy for My Grandmother in the Form of a Cactus

The way each linked lobe of your cactus swallows all
the green from the one before it reminds me of that movie
about the human centipede and how appalled you'd have been
to know such a film exists, though you were no stranger
to the macabre, you who used to warn me not to drink tea
too much or my stomach would swell red, you said,
citing the story of that man with the shotgun wound
in his abdomen, how he became a medical curiosity
for the dark deep hole in him through which the world
could suddenly view the innermost sanctum of a human body,
which was a long way you had of saying it matters what we put
inside ourselves. I have put so many things inside myself I should
not have: smoke of all sorts, whiskey, sorrow, pennies, bottomless
guilt, river stones, a crusty work glove pulled off with my teeth.
I even licked a Burmese python once on a dare. I list the contraband
of my body to myself as I eat nachos or frozen French fries
off your blue dinner plates, counting the indulgences
I imagine you would not have approved. And here I am
inserting a gross horror movie reference into a poem
about your absence, a poem I began writing only because
I wanted you to know: your cactus is flowering again,
as it has for four years now, fuchsia flames licking out
from the maw of each final green—I don't know what to call it,
not a leaf, but a section of stem pressed flat—until yes,
it erupts into firework, a tongue or tail of brightness uncurling
into this winter room. I wanted you to know: it flowered
the night you died. It flowered because I told it to,
you in your hospital bed and me not there. And now

I force it unconsciously each year, forget to water
for months then soak it with the thawed remains
of yesterday's chicken pail. It's an Easter cactus really,
I wanted you to know. I looked it up on a diagram today—
the three shapes of lobe—but yours is willful, peculiar, blooms
only in late January, blooms only for you. Which is fitting,
since we don't believe in resurrection, you or I. Just another
flattened green segment each year, another stubborn
explosion of beauty at the end of our grief.

Blessing for the End Times

We can't stop counting backwards & why not? Tonight's moon, blood-
blistering her eclipse as our necks crane starward, should be answer

enough. Between threat & prayer, what lisps & winks like night
between our bodies, circling us on the lawn, mapping breath & distance—

it's like the looped trick knot on the grain sack; with the right pull
we all come undone, an ellipsis of string uncoiling to let loose

what we need. Which is either hope or a destination, depending
who you ask. Me? I need this glinting asterism above & all its

brightly studded teeth. Your lips with their warmth & tender.
I need every unnamed pocked riverbed on every planet I'll never visit

& some days I need to pretend I am a sweater woven of only a single
strand & one end is slipped around your wrist & the other is tied

to the black hole in the middle of the galaxy, that newly photographed
abscess thrilling all the astronomers with its sphincter of promise

& schism. Like this morning when you stood naked & flossing
at the sink & I saw a white cat slink your ankles & knew it was a dream

so I told you & we walked hand in hand to the slipshod front step
where we leapt into the air only to find flying is like swimming,

our bodies suddenly weightless but suspended at the threshold
of descent—unless in motion—unless we glided our hands behind us

as oars, slicing currents of shadow while fear hissed its soothing helium
into our lungs, transporting us foot by slow foot into the slipstream.

Death Fluorescence

This is how the body unfurls itself into death: blue cascade, black light waterfall,
     lava lamp of weeping. The worms writhe under their demise, shudder

six hours of bursting skylines, their dying an epidemic of cells exploding
     in bluet, bluebonnet, whole fields of cornflower or hydrangea. In school

I learned my blood was cobalt inside my body—until finger sliced,
     until exposed to air—an erroneous conviction that lingers stubbornly—

this notion of transformation by pain. A death wave, scientists call it.
     Lysosomes burst, one cell eats itself and then the next until whole villages

are demolished inside the worm, each fatality a flash-bang,
     a blinding cerulean destruction you can diagram now on a screen, study live

along with the researchers—you, a drone operator surveying the town square
     before pressing the detonation button. Watch the world blast itself apart

into gas fire, dart frog, the oceanic rippling mouth of the maxima clam,
     its tidal heaving. You needn't look far. Everywhere another thrashing collapse

nested inside another, each tinier than the last: a matryoshka
     of death propagation, a colonization of extinction. Night the same

inside any animal, exhaling from the epicenter into ever more brilliant shades.
     Didn't you always want a blueprint for your own annihilation? Well here it is,

beautiful one: you are a Bunsen burner, an orchard budding azure flames,
     two leopard slugs entwined upside-down on their helixed rope of mucus

as their alien-blue penises unravel from the sides of their heads,
     an intimate twirl that spins and spins like light through blown glass.

Within you is an entire universe of starry luminescent decay—a web-work
     of indigo highways connecting each galaxy to another where there is nothing

left to do but step forward, step out into ocean, gemstone, peacock, dragonfly,
     planet, ribbon eel, this horizon you are and are not yet without.

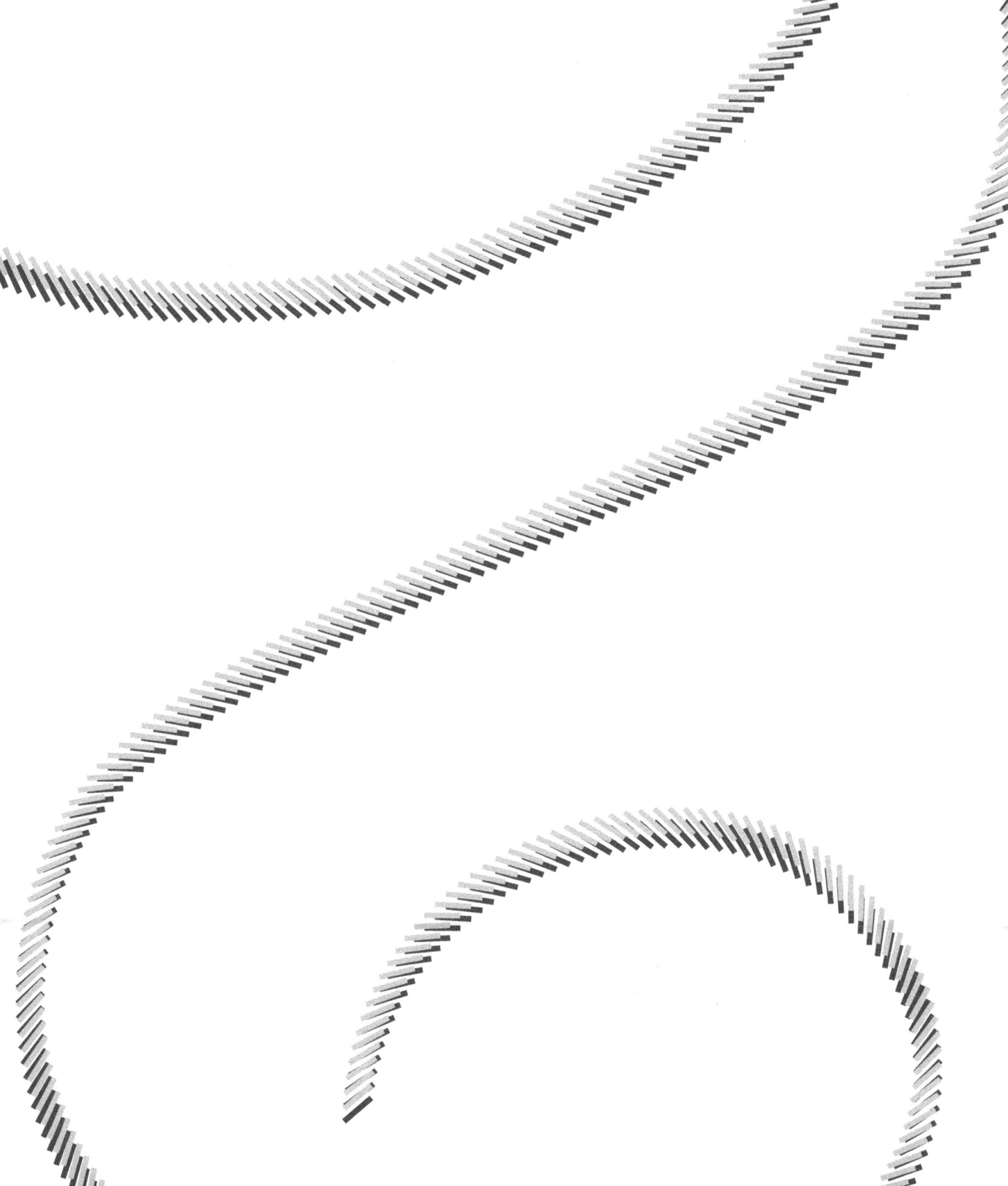

Notes

"Etymology of Land" was written in conversation with Don West's *Clods of Southern Earth*. I was inspired to the etymology form by reading Kristin Chang's "Etymology of Butch."

"After We Wound the Land to Maps" is after Franny Choi's "The World Keeps Ending, and the World Goes On."

"A Meditation on Parasitic Infection": The prefatory note for this poem quotes a line from the *Parasitipedia.net* entry for *Ascaris suum*.

"Study in Epigenetic Memory: A Memory of Warmth" was inspired by reading the 2018 *Science Alert* article "Scientists Have Observed Epigenetic Memories Being Passed Down for 14 Generations."

"I'm Okay, but the Country Is Not": This sonnet crown is dedicated to the memory of my grandmother, Gloria Robinson (February 20, 1924 - January 30, 2017), author of *Prelude to Genetics: Theories of a Material Substance of Heredity—Darwin to Weismann*.

    The third sonnet in this sequence quotes lines from Thomas Carlyle's poem "Today."

    The fourth sonnet in this sequence quotes a line from William Ernest Henley's poem "Invictus."

    The sixth sonnet in this sequence quotes a phrase from Gloria Robinson's *Prelude to Genetics*.

    The lines "a hole is for digging" (twelfth sonnet) and "a tablespoon is for eating tables with" (ninth sonnet) are from the 1952 children's book *A Hole Is to Dig: A First Book of First Definitions* by Ruth Krauss with illustrations by Maurice Sendak.

"Study in Epigenetic Memory: The Neurosis Persists" was inspired by reading the 2019 *BBC* article by Martha Henriques entitled "Can the legacy of trauma be passed down for generations?"

"Muscle Memory: A Surgery" is composed of eight different erasures using the same source text: surgical notes written by pediatric ophthalmologist Dr. Jeffrey Berman after performing a bilateral strabismus surgery on me in June 2022, a surgery initially recommended for me at age twelve and which I instead received at age forty-two.

"Small-Town Parade / Frozen Lake: Notes on Fear" draws on various acupuncture blog posts, as well as the *Yellow Emperor's Classic of Medicine* by Maoshing Ni.

"Drought Diary" quotes a line from Diana Khoi Nguyen's poem "A Bird in Chile, and Elsewhere," published in *Ghost Of* (Omnidawn, 2018).

"I Have No Answer but Stones" quotes from the diary of Yitzchak Rudashevski as excerpted on the Yad Vashem website. Further diary entries can be found in *Salvaged Bones: Young Writers' Diaries of the Holocaust*, collected and edited by Alexandra Zapruder (Yale University Press, 2002).

"A Catalog of Endlings" quotes Eric Freedman's "Cut from History: An Abandoned Tasmanian Zoo Tells the Haunting Tale of an Endling" (*EJ Magazine,* July 2008) and draws on information and language from his "Extinction is Forever: A Quest for the Last Known Survivors" (*Earth Island Journal*, 2011).

"Home Movie with Storm, Orchard, and News": This poem is written as a Markov Sonnet, a form invented by Palestinian American poet George Abraham and inspired by the Markov Chain. Abraham describes the form as "a sonnet where every set of 3 lines is to be read in isolation (abc / bcd / cde /...) as a cause/action/effect triplet; the poem both aggressively forgets itself & repeats, much like history."

   This poem also references a film taken by my great-grandfather. Wolf Rabinowitz, son of Tuvia and Frida Rabinowitz of Mažeikiai, Lithuania (then in Czarist Russia), emigrated to the United States in 1915. There he adopted the name William Robinson, became a doctor of radiology, married Edna Kurzrok and started a family. In July 1928, bringing an early movie camera, he returned to visit his family in Mažeikiai, then in independent Lithuania. William Robinson's brothers Yosef, Samuel, Lejb and their families later perished in the Holocaust after the German invasion of Lithuania in June 1941.

"What Will You Do at the End of the World?" was inspired by watching the YouTube video of violist Dagmar Turner playing as surgeons at a London hospital operated to remove her brain tumor in 2020.

"Study in Epigenetic Memory: Flower and Petal" draws on an epigenetics experiment described in the 2013 *New Scientist* article "Fear of a smell can be passed down several generations."

Acknowledgments

Grateful acknowledgment is made to the following publications in which these poems appear, often in earlier versions:

Cutthroat	"Hiraeth" "Sugaring at the Start of Another War" "I Have No Answer but Stones"
Ecotone	"Blessing for the End Times"
Green Mountains Review	"A Meditation on Parasitic Infection" *(as "Study in Epigenetic Memory")* "What Will You Do at the End of the World?"
Ilanot Review	"Blood and Soil"
Kenyon Review	"After We Wound the Land to Maps" "Drought Diary"
Maine Arts Journal	"The Thing About Fire"
PLUME	"Elegy for My Grandmother in the Form of a Cactus"
Poems from Here (Maine Public)	"What Will You Do at the End of the World?"
The Shore	"Study in Epigenetic Memory: Flower and Petal" *(as "Study in Epigenetic Memory")*

"Etymology of Land" is included in *What Things Cost: an anthology for the people,* edited by Rebecca Gayle Howell and Ashley M. Jones, and Emily Jalloul. University Press of Kentucky, 2023.

"I Have No Answer but Stones," "What Will You Do at the End of the World?," and "Elegy for My Grandmother in the Form of a Cactus" also appear on poets.org.

"To a Mainer Living 100 years from Now" was written at the request of the Maine Arts Commission and included in a time capsule for Maine's bicentennial celebration. The time capsule will be opened in 2120. The Maine Arts commission also created a video of the poem.

The thirteenth sonnet in "I'm Okay, but the Country Is Not" *[Bring your shovel. Wherever we go, there'll be music there—]* was set to music as part of the extended choral piece "the dark and marvelous way" (2024) by composer Hilary Purrington.

Many thanks to Monson Arts for the gift of a residency during which the first draft of this book came to life. To A CLEARING for the A POSSIBLE PRACTICE cycles that have inspired several of these poems. And to Maine Writers & Publishers Alliance for your incredible support of my work along with that of so many Maine writers.

My gratitude to everyone at Sundress Publications, and especially to Krista Cox, for bringing this book into the world with so much care and support.

Thank you to Lee Horikoshi Roripaugh and Sean Thomas Dougherty for your generous words in support of this book, and for the powerful inspiration you have provided me through your own work.

Thank you to Shaindel Beers, Sara Borjas, Lexie Bouwsma, Cynthia Dewi Oka, and Ada Wofford for reading various drafts of this book, at different stages in its development. Your advice and encouragement allowed me to push this project further than I ever could have on my own.

To my friends. My teachers. My family born and found. To everyone who has held me in community, literary or otherwise. Everyone who has supported me through this work. Who has literally held me in your arms. There are too many of you to name, but know that I see each and every one of you.

To my great-grandmother. My grandmothers. My mother. My sister. Thank you for the paths you have set. Without them I would not have found my own.

And to Walker—there is no one I would rather walk beside, no matter how thin the earth's crust.

About the Author

Julia Bouwsma lives off-the-grid in the mountains of western Maine where she is a poet, homesteader, editor, teacher, and small-town librarian, as well as Maine's sixth Poet Laureate, serving a term from 2021 to 2026. Bouwsma is the author of three poetry collections: *Death Fluorescence* (Sundress Publications, 2025), *Midden* (Fordham University Press, 2018), and *Work by Bloodlight* (Cider Press Review, 2017). She is also the librettist for the short chamber opera, *Ghost Apples*, created in collaboration with composer Nathan Davis and the Halcyon Quartet. A recipient of a 2024 Poet Laureate Fellowship from the Academy of American Poets and two Maine Literary Awards, Bouwsma serves as Library Director for Webster Library in Kingfield, Maine.

Other Sundress Titles

Pork Fluff
Tiffany Hsieh
$17.95

Still My Father's Son
Nora Hikari
$17.95

The Parachutist
Jose Hernandez Diaz
$16

Pure Fear, American Legend
Laura Dzubay
$20

Florence
Bess Cooley
$16

Spoke the Dark Matter
Michelle Whittaker
$16

DANGEROUS BODIES/ANGER ODES
stevie redwood
$16

Good Son
Kyle Liang
$16

Back to Alabama
Valerie A. Smith
$16

Slaughterhouse for Old Wives Tales
Hannah V Warren
$16

Grief Slut
Evelyn Berry
$16

Nocturne in Joy
Tatiana Johnson-Boria
$16

Ruin & Want
José Angel Araguz
$20

Age of Forgiveness
Caleb Curtiss
$16

Another Word for Hunger
Heather Bartlett
$16

www.ingramcontent.com/pod-product-compliance
Lightning Source LLC
Chambersburg PA
CBHW061115170426
43198CB00026B/2992